HISTORIC FORTS
of
MICHIGAN

DAVID WEDGE

Published by The History Press
An imprint of Arcadia Publishing
Charleston, SC
www.historypress.com

First published 2026

Manufactured in the United States

ISBN 9781467170079

Library of Congress Control Number: 2025945979

CONTENTS

PREFACE

I have always been interested in military stuff. I come from a long line of military men. I am a U.S. Air Force veteran of the Vietnam War. I grew up in Port Huron, Michigan, so I always knew about Fort St. Joseph and Fort Gratiot. I graduated from Lake Superior State University, so I also knew about the two Fort Bradys, along with Fort Mackinac and Michilimackinac. I was pretty sure that there must be others, but I did not know what and where they were. So I went to the local public library and started doing research on other Michigan forts. At the library, I found out that there was no singular book on the subject. Over the ensuing years, life kind of got in the way of research and writing. I had a family to support and a job to do. The fort project got pushed to the back of the closet for a number of years. I never really forgot about it, but I did not always have much time to give it.

When I retired, I pulled out the fort research material and my notes and began the process of reading and rewriting some of it while also making numerous trips to the fort sites. I had spent an inordinate amount of time in public libraries and small museums looking for the most obscure references to any military fortification. The vast majority of my research took place before the advent of the internet. But the internet has been most helpful with the job of verifying my earlier research.

In the beginning, my research was only to satisfy my personal need to know about military forts built on Michigan soil prior to 1837 statehood. It was only later, when my family and friends suggested that I should actually try to get it published, that I started to give that any serious thought.

It took a long time to find a publisher. By way of historian Dianna Stampfler, I received an introduction to The History Press and Arcadia Publishing. It was the answer to a prayer.

This book is dedicated to my supportive and patient wife and to my intelligent, gifted daughter. The book would not have been possible without their support and assistance.

INTRODUCTION

Throughout the history of the Great Lakes region in general and Michigan in particular, the militaries of various European nations have played a vital role in its exploration and eventual settlement. With the arrival of the first French explorer in North America in 1534 and until Michigan was admitted into the Union in 1837, the military forces of four different countries have laid claim to the territory. Aside from the Native American cultures that lived and died on Michigan soil and the early American pioneers who do currently occupy the land, the nations of France, Spain, and Great Britain have all laid claim to some or all of Michigan at one time or another.

The evidence of their presence here is all around us. The names of our lakes, rivers, cities, and streets are proof of their early presence. With the physical evidence left behind in their settlements and the written records they kept, we can trace their steps and understand their motives for movement throughout the region.

The history of Michigan forts that were built prior to 1837 statehood is a fascinating subject by which we can measure the adventurous spirit, the religious dedication, and, in some cases, the tremendous greed of those early European explorers. The overwhelming desire for the accumulation of wealth through the vast resources of the New World brought a swift and devastating end to the ancient lifestyles of the proud Native Americans and sparked renewed and fierce rivalries between European nations for control of this new empire, rivalries that have been part of the European continent for one thousand years.

Those age-old rivalries still have a behind-the-curtain shuffling of foreign policies with regard to North America. The very fact that Canada was not made part of the United States during the treaty negotiations to end the War of 1812 has never been completely understood by historians, then and now. A plan for the Canadian wilderness and its vast natural resources was never actually developed by the British beyond scooping up as much of the natural resources as they could. Their hold on the vast wilderness of North America had been tenuous at best, but that weak connection was never politically tested by the American negotiators until after that final boundary line was placed.

Many Americans believed at the time the Treaty of Ghent was being negotiated that the northern boundaries of New York, Vermont, New Hampshire, and Maine should have been extended to the St. Lawrence Seaway and that U.S. territory should also have included New Brunswick, Prince Edward Island, and Nova Scotia.

The study of Michigan forts can best be accomplished by understanding the motives of the early explorers to penetrate farther and farther into the interior of North America. The French, in particular, with their trading posts and military encampments placed in strategic locations—by which they could control hundreds of miles of lakes and rivers—were vitally important to the early exploration and later settlement of the Great Lakes region.

In the early days of exploration, travel was either by way of following old Native American trails or by water. By locating the forts at the headwaters of major rivers and at the conflux of lakes, the French controlled the fur trade for 150 years, allowing only the occasional foreign trapper and trader to sneak through their defenses.

Explorers such as Champlain, Nicolet, and La Salle; religious men like Marquette, Raymbault, Mesnard, and Hennepin; and the military leadership of Gladwin, Sinclair, DuLuth, Cadillac, Champlain, and Wolfe, to name just a few, all played important and valuable roles for their nations to obtain and maintain control of the vast North American territories.

Of the twenty military installations that were built on Michigan soil prior to 1837 statehood, fourteen of them were a direct result of the fierce and bitter rivalry between the French and English to control the region, with the Spanish also getting a temporary toehold in the southwest corner of "the Mitten."

In order that the reader might better understand the reason for the location of some forts, a brief history of the exploration of the Great Lakes region and the changing relations between Native Americans and the Europeans is included here.

I hope the reader will find this book as fun and interesting to read as it was to research and write.

Part I

EXPLORATION AND SETTLEMENT OF MICHIGAN AND THE GREAT LAKES REGION

Native American history and active settlement of what would later become Michigan quite probably began as early as 15,000 BC, when the last glacier of the Labradorian Glacial Age, which had sat dormant for one thousand years of subzero temperatures, began to melt.

Over the eons of its formation, the planet has gone through multiple periods of warming and cooling, leading to millions of years of continual weather changes. Climate change has always been a part of the history of this planet, a part of the cycle and recycled weather dynamics of our earthly home.

Nearly fifty thousand years ago, the Labradorian glacier moved down from northern Canada, pushing huge rock formations, boulders, and vast miles of dirt in front of it. At its most southerly point, the glacier reached to where the Ohio River flows today. It melted slowly at first, sitting dormant for one thousand years; after Earth rotated on its axis less than one degree, it started melting more swiftly—at least swiftly in terms of epochs. The glacier gradually pulled back north as its southern leading edge continued to melt, creating what we today call the Great Lakes. The melting of the glacier eventually stalled and then stopped in its current location just north of James Bay and the Hudson Bay. It melts and then refreezes through the seasons and has continued as one of the feeder troughs of fresh water into the Great Lakes system.

Native American peoples slowly followed the glacier northward into what would become the Michigan territory, where they established small fishing villages as they learned how to survive in the northern climate, where mighty mastodon roamed. Evidence continues to be uncovered and dug up to show conclusively that the large animals were regularly stalked and killed by Native Americans. The evidence is clear that the Native Americans and the mastodon did coexist in Michigan.

Native Americans followed game animals as the animals moved with the seasons. Migratory birds flooding into the Great Lakes on their flights north and south were always a welcome sight to the Native people. They studied the patterns of bird migration and learned how to hunt and trap them successfully. The Native people hunted the deer and elk and used the skins for clothing and shelter. The process of using the brain tissue from the skull of the animal to properly tan the hide was learned over many generations. The Natives discovered a wild "rice-like" plant with nutritional benefits and learned how to cultivate the plant. The Native people taught themselves how to weave natural material into baskets and set the baskets in rivers and streams to catch fish.

Many of the tasks of everyday life were learned by Native peoples over many generations going back to when North America was first populated. Many anthropologists believe that "people" first entered the North American continent by crossing the "land bridge" when the Bering Sea was frozen between northern Russia and Alaska some ten-thousand-plus years ago. However, the argument for that migration is far from settled, as there is significant evidence in White Sands National Park in the New Mexico desert to suggest that at the time of the frozen land bridge, there had already been humans living on the continent for many thousands of years, evidence that simply cannot be refuted.

Europeans have been active in North America longer than most historians originally thought. There is evidence of European activity that has recently been uncovered on Oak Island in Nova Scotia's Mahone Bay to suggest European contact going back as far as the early 1400s. It has been suggested that it was mostly pirate activity, but that evidence is, as yet, inconclusive.

What we do know about the European discovery of North America, in documented evidence, is that as early as 1506, there were Frenchmen fishing off the coast of present-day Newfoundland. But for some unknown reason, those early fishermen were not at all interested in exploring this unknown land or in trading with its inhabitants.

The French finally landed in North America in 1534 when Jacques Cartier sailed from France in command of two ships and explored around the mouth of the St. Lawrence River. In 1535, he returned to North America and sailed up the St. Lawrence River as far as present-day Montreal. Cartier and his men spent the winter at an Indian camp that is now Quebec City and endured months of bitter cold and suffering. Many men died of scurvy, caused by the lack of fresh food. When spring arrived, Cartier and what was left of his men sped home to France.

The stories told by Cartier of the long, hard winter in this new land did not discourage the adventurous spirit of the French. They were, in fact, encouraged. The tales of Cartier sparked a burning interest and desire for adventure and discovery that would eventually bring fame to some and fortune to others, but rarely did one person get both.

Probably around 1606, a full ten years before the Pilgrims landed at Plymouth Rock, the first white man to set foot on what is now Michigan soil was a young Frenchman named Etienné Brulé. He had been sent by Champlain to live with the Native Americans and learn their way of life and language. Just eighteen years old at the time, he accompanied a group of Natives through what would become known as the Sault Ste. Marie rapids and waterway. After a short foray of exploring the area, he returned to Quebec with a nugget of pure copper and tales of a large freshwater sea that lay to the west, referring to what we now know as Lake Superior.

Wanting to see this large sea for himself and believing it might be the route to what was then called the Orient, Champlain began a journey overland from Quebec that took him into Georgian Bay and then into upper Lake Huron. This was the first of the Great Lakes to be discovered by Champlain. On the same trip, Champlain discovered Lake Ontario by moving south from northern Lake Huron across land, through what is now the province of Ontario. Why Champlain did not go northwest to the large freshwater sea described by Brulé may never be known. His letters and diaries do not include any reference to the large freshwater sea to the northwest.

Other Frenchmen came to North America, which was then referred to as New France, to establish settlements. No other French settlements at the time were as well-known as Quebec. Samuel Champlain began his stay at Quebec in 1608. Champlain's intention was to establish a fur trade with the Native Americans. The first winter Champlain spent at Quebec was very hard and discouraging. He realized that Cartier's tales were not exaggerated.

In June 1609, more men and provisions arrived at the French colony. That same month, a band of more than three hundred Huron and Ottawa Natives, collectively called Algonquins by Champlain, arrived at Quebec. The Algonquins were planning to attack their enemy, the Iroquois, who lived to the south in what would later become New York State. The Algonquins wanted Champlain and his men to aid them in their attack by bringing their strange, powerful weapon, the gun.

Champlain, wanting to explore the region farther up the St. Lawrence River, agreed to help his new Native friends. Champlain, his men, and the Native war party went up the river as far as the Richelieu River, where the Natives began quarreling among themselves, whereupon more than half of them left the war party and returned to their homes. In spite of this, Champlain continued on the journey.

The war party moved slowly south on the Richelieu River and advanced on the Iroquois very carefully. On July 4, 1609, Champlain and the war party discovered a large lake that had never been seen by white men. Champlain named it Lake Champlain in honor of himself. As they continued southward, the war party finally made contact with the Iroquois on July 30.

Had Champlain known more about the different bands of Native Americans, he probably would not have helped the Algonquins. Had he known that the Iroquois were the strongest and the most warlike of all Natives in eastern North America, he would surely have gone to great lengths to cultivate their friendship.

The Iroquois were strong and brave but did not stand a chance against the muskets of Champlain. They had never heard the roar of gunfire, yet they held their ground and got off a strong volley of arrows at the intruders. Again the loud weapons sounded, belching smoke and fire, and this time the Iroquois ran in panic. They were followed quickly by the victorious Algonquins, and many Iroquois were killed.

This battle, fought on the shore of Lake Champlain near where Old Fort Ticonderoga stands, had a great impact on the later history of North America. The only historical significance of the actual battle is that it bound the Algonquins in friendship to the French and turned the Iroquois into bitter enemies of the French. The story of that first battle was handed down from father to son among the Iroquois, and many times during the following years they attacked the little French settlement along the St. Lawrence and killed many French men, along with women and children.

Just two months after that battle, a Dutch ship appeared on a waterway that would later be named the Hudson River. The ship was the *Half Moon*, belonging to Henry Hudson. It was soon followed by other Dutch ships wanting to trade with the Indians. A strong friendship developed between the Dutch and the Iroquois. The Dutch gave them firearms in exchange for furs, and the Indians were again able to meet their old enemies the Algonquins in battle as equals.

There were two solid reasons for the French to be attracted to North America. First, the woods and rivers provided many fur-bearing animals that would bring large amounts of money to those who braved the wilderness. Second was the desire of the Jesuits and the many Frenchmen to save the souls of the "heathen" Native American tribes. For these two reasons, the French traders and missionaries were the first white men to come to the Great Lakes region. The slow and devastating downfall of virtually every Native tribe in North America had begun.

When the French first arrived in North America, the Natives were living a very simple life, using only such things as they found around their villages. Rarely did they roam far from their tribal lands, but from the time the French arrived, the Natives became less and less independent. They relied heavily on the French for blankets, clothing, guns, gunpowder, and alcohol. Unfortunately, it was the alcohol more than anything else that became one of the chief components of their ruin.

To get the French goods, the Natives were required to secure an ever-increasing amount of furs to trade with. The increase in hunting for more furs did much to break up old tribal locations and break down Native lifestyles. They became great rovers and were often found far from their traditional lands. Native life in North American had taken its first and fateful steps into the future and would never again be the same.

Champlain, growing old and busy with government affairs, left the further exploration of the Great Lakes region to younger men. In 1634, Jean Nicolet turned north out of Lake Huron and went up the St. Mary's River to the rapids where the city of Sault Ste. Marie now stands. Returning south, Nicolet discovered the Straits of Mackinac and the large humped piece of land we now call Mackinac Island. Going westward, he discovered Lake Michigan and Green Bay. Some historians believe that he also went as far southwest at the headwaters of the Mississippi River, but Nicolet made no mention of this in his records.

The work of the Jesuit missionaries in trying to convert the Natives to Christianity is one of the most interesting stories in all the history of North America and played a large part in the settlement of Michigan. The missionaries faced incredible hardships of bitter weather and dangerous journeys through the wilderness for no real material gain. They had to learn how to travel along the many rivers and through miles and miles of seemingly endless forests to reach the Native encampments, while also needing to forage for food and defending themselves from the hungry forest animals like bears and wolves.

In 1641, two Jesuit missionaries, Father Raymbault and Father Jogues, arrived at the St. Mary's River rapids, which they called the "Sault," a French word meaning "to skip" or "jump." Here they found a Native settlement of more than two thousand people. The Jesuits were greeted warmly and invited to stay at the village, but they decided to continue on their journey west. Due to the hardships of the wilderness, Father Raymbault became ill and died the following year. Father Jogues was later tortured and killed by the Iroquois.

In 1660, Father Rene Mesnard set out on a westward journey from Quebec. Going up the St. Mary's River and rapids, he entered Lake Superior and followed its southern shore to Keeweenau Bay. There he established the first Jesuit mission in North America.

In 1667, Father Jacques Marquette and Father Claude Dablon were sent into the Upper Great Lakes region to convert Native Americans to Christianity. Upon arriving at the St. Mary's River rapids, they started a mission that later became the French settlement of Sault Ste. Marie, the oldest continuous European settlement in Michigan.

Father Marquette traveled throughout the Upper Peninsula and the Lake Michigan area extensively, learning all he could of Native American life. Upon returning to Sault Ste. Marie, Marquette learned that a large number of Huron tribe members had gathered at Michilimackinac. (The name is of a general nature, referring not to a settlement or fort but rather to the entire area around the Straits of Mackinac. Only later was this name applied to the French fort on the southern tip of the Straits of Mackinac.) Marquette traveled to the Michilimackinac Straits in 1671, where he founded a mission and named it St. Ignatius, which is now the city of St. Ignace. In 1672, the French military arrived at St. Ignace and built Fort DuBuade, along with a trading post.

The work of the traders, missionaries, and skilled cartographers had progressed such that by 1669, a fairly accurate map of the Upper Lakes region had been made. The French wished to take advantage of the friendship offered them by Native tribes of the region so they could hold in check the English fur traders who had formed the Hudson Bay Company. With their knowledge of the region, through their continuous exploration, the French were able to do this for many years.

The task of establishing French authority over the fur trading business in the Upper Midwest fell on Simon François Daumont. He arrived at Sault Ste. Marie with fifteen men in May 1671. A call was immediately sent out to the Native tribes for delegates to attend a council. Fourteen tribes responded by sending delegates to the Sault to represent them at the council. This strange meeting was held in the wilderness on the banks of the St. Mary's River. It was attended by the Native delegates, French fur traders, the black-robed Jesuits, and French officers representing the king.

Many speeches were made. A large cross was erected, and also a large post was raised on which the Arms of France was placed. Thus, France, in 1671, took formal possession of the Upper Great Lakes region. An interesting sidenote here is that the French legal claims to the land around present-day Sault Ste. Marie were not complete or final until a Supreme Court decision was handed down years after the American Civil War ended.

After the death of Father Marquette in 1675, a Frenchman named La Salle, who was also called "the Dreamer," known for his exploratory work, arrived in New France with many grand ideas. He learned from the Natives that to the south of Lake Erie there was a river that flowed south to a large saltwater sea. The sea was so far away that it could be reached only after many months in a canoe.

La Salle, thinking that he may have learned of the "passage way to China," for which many explorers were still searching, learned all he could from the Natives about the river leading to the sea. He went south from Lake Erie and found the Ohio River, following it to where Louisville, Kentucky, now stands. He returned to the Upper Lakes with hopes of winning the entire region for France. The reasons for the decision to turn back before reaching the saltwater sea may never be known. La Salle's records during this period are incomplete or lost.

La Salle had materials for a sailboat sent to Lake Erie. On the shore of Lake Erie, near where Buffalo, New York, now stands, the *Griffin* was built. This was to be the first sailing vessel ever to ply the waters of the Great Lakes.

In the spring of 1679, La Salle guided the *Griffin* up the Detroit River and into Lake St. Clair. On board the *Griffin* was a priest named Father Hennepin. When the *Griffin* first reached the small lake at the north end of the Detroit River, the French were celebrating the French Catholic "Feast of the Ste. Claire." Father Hennepin thought this significant enough to name this body of water Lake St. Clair. The *Griffin* then continued to sail up into Lake Huron and on to the Straits of Mackinac.

La Salle then sailed through the Straits of Mackinac to present-day Green Bay, Wisconsin, where he traded with Natives, bought furs from other traders, and loaded the boat with other cargo. He then set sail for the east side of Lake Michigan to the St. Joseph River. La Salle and his men began the construction of a fort at the mouth of the St. St. Joseph River. It was the very first fort ever built on Michigan soil that was strictly for defensive purposes. With the fort complete, La Salle assigned some of his men to sail the *Griffin* back to Niagara Falls, offload the furs, and then return to Fort Miami to pick up La Salle and the other men, who volunteered to stay behind to trade with the Natives. The *Griffin* did not make the return trip back to the St. Joseph River, and there is no evidence that the sailing ship even made it to Lake Erie.

The *Griffin*, after leaving La Salle and part of its crew behind, headed out across Lake Michigan. The mystery of its disappearance has never been solved. Many theories have been put forth, such as Native Americans capturing and burning it or that it was the victim of a sudden and violent Great Lakes storm. La Salle believed to his dying day that the crew stole the valuable furs and then destroyed the ship to cover up the theft. The disappearance of the *Griffin* is as much a mystery now as it was then. No evidence to verify its demise has ever been found.

Fort DuBuade, during its lifetime, became the most important of all French posts in the Upper Great Lakes region. This was due to its strategic location on the Straits of Mackinac (which connects Lakes Huron and Michigan and with the St. Mary's River), a short distance from the outlet of Lake Superior, and near the Ottawa River, the main route to Montreal and Quebec.

As the years passed, the small outposts in the Great Lakes region grew in importance. The endless demand for furs caused the Native American and French trappers to push farther and farther west, where game was more abundant. Gradually, the French established more fortified forts to hold their power over the region and keep the Natives and English in check.

Other posts were also important from time to time. Fort Miami, Fort St. Joseph at Niles, Fort St. Joseph at Port Huron, and the settlement at Sault Ste. Marie all had their day in the sun.

In 1686, Daniel DuLuth built the first Fort St. Joseph, where Port Huron stands today, at the north end of the St. Clair River, where Lake Huron dumps its water. The purpose of the fort was to keep the English out of the Upper Lakes region.

Between Kaskaskia and Cahokia, on the Mississippi River, the French had also built Fort Chartres to help hold the Mississippi Valley and protect the river route to New Orleans. All the French forts were built in the palisaded style and guarded only by a small company of soldiers.

The forts of the day were usually one of three kinds. The simplest was an enclosure formed by a stockade of vertical logs. A narrow trench was dug three or four feet deep. Logs from twelve to fifteen feet in length were placed in it vertically, and earth was tamped around them. Loopholes would then be cut through the logs so they could be secured together with rope. Then barracks and storehouses were constructed inside the walls.

The second type of fort was a modification of the original style and was built when they had sufficient time. The construct called for the meeting faces of the logs to be flattened and snugged together horizontally so no enemy bullets could pass through. This fort could be efficiently defended and was quite safe from an attack that did not employ artillery. Cannons, however, could make short work of this type of stockade.

The third and strongest type of fort was made by building walls of timber cribbing, filled with earth and faced with timber. This provided an excellent defense against artillery. The disadvantage to this type of fort was that before many years had passed the timber on the bottom would rot and the fort walls would collapse.

All forts usually followed the same type of floor plan, either that of a square or of a five-pointed star, with redoubts extending out from each corner to allow flanking fire along the length of the walls between the redoubts.

In time, the rivalry between the French and English grew stronger. The English came into the region and offered the Native Americans more rum for their furs than the French were offering. The English also offered other supplies in greater quantities, but of lower quality. Little by little, the Natives began trading more furs with the English, and by 1700, the French were forced to establish another fort to protect their fur trade.

In 1701, Antoine de la Mothe Cadillac, the French commander at Fort DuBuade at present-day St. Ignace, moved the majority of his garrison south to where Detroit now stands. Here on the banks of the "River de Troit" (Detroit River) he built a new fort and named it Fort Pontchartrain in honor of Count Pontchartrain, the French diplomat who gave him permission and the funds to build the new fort.

Other French settlers came to the area and established farms. Then Natives of the Huron, Miami, and Ottawa and Ojibwa tribes began to gather around the fort. They came seeking protection from the Iroquois. Cadillac's settlement was called "Ville de Troit," meaning "village of the straits." Later, the word *village* was dropped, and the settlement became known simply as Detroit.

As Detroit grew in size and importance, Fort DuBuade at St. Ignace was deserted. When Cadillac left the fort and moved south to establish his new settlement at Detroit, most of the traders and Natives followed him. Three years later, the Jesuits closed their mission at St. Ignace, burned the chapel, and also left the Mackinac Straits area. It would not be many years before the Straits of Mackinac would regain much of its former importance to the region.

IN 1710, WITH REPORTS of theft, bribery, and incompetence, the king of France made Cadillac the governor of Louisiana, and Cadillac left the Great Lakes region, never to return. His name has been used for the brand of a luxury automobile, and a mid-Michigan city was named in his honor.

Traders with illegal goods on unlicensed canoes began gathering at the Straits of Michilimackinac, on the northern tip of the Lower Peninsula just west of present-day Mackinaw City. By 1713, the French had built a new fort called Fort Michilimackinac to control the trade and amount of brandy flowing to the Native Americans.

The regulations for granting a license to trade with the Natives varied from post to post and also with the nation in power at the time. In 1746, under French control, the cost of a license was 400 francs (approximately $100), plus the stipulation that each canoe carry an additional five hundred pounds of goods for the king.

By 1757, a trading license cost 600 francs ($300) per canoe, and each was required to carry eight hundred pounds of goods. The canoes were sturdily made, generally of birch or elm bark, and were large enough to hold from two to fourteen paddlers in addition to the cargo.

The smallest canoes were manned by three men and could carry as much as 2,300 pounds of cargo, yet they were so light that one person could carry an empty one over the portages.

By 1748, the French government had sensed its growing weakness in its rivalry with the English in North America. It tried to encourage French settlers to come to the Great Lakes region with the offer of plows, wagons, and other agricultural tools, plus land grants. But France had waited too long to develop these resources in the region.

At the outbreak of the French and Indian War in America and the Seven Years' War in Europe, many Frenchmen and Native Americans left the Michilimackinac and Detroit areas to help fight in the war in the East.

When British General Wolfe defeated French General Montcalm, the fortress at Quebec fell into English hands. The English then marched on and took Montreal. The French surrender was a dramatic and historically important event. After 150 years of French control, New France was suddenly, but temporarily, the property of the English king.

What did the English get when they took control of the territory? A land rich in copper deposits worth more than any Englishman could dream of, a land rich in iron ore beyond their wildest imaginations, and a land filled from shore to shore with majestic white pine that would eventually yield an incalculable number of board feet and make many people very wealthy. They got all this, but instead they were looking for furs and could not see where the real value was.

The English had legal title to this land for twenty-two years and held on stubbornly for another six years after losing it to the upstart Americans first in the Revolution and then again in the War of 1812. For that entire twenty-eight-year period, the English eyes saw only the fur-bearing animals.

Yet the greatest tragedy of all was that the English could not see the value of the knowledge held by Native Americans. Believing themselves to be far superior, the English treated the Natives with contempt and considered them a nuisance. This led to hard and bitter feelings and then to outright hatred. The tragedy lies in all the unnecessary suffering and killing that, for the most part, could have been avoided.

The many ancient tribal lifestyles of the Native Americans are now nearly gone, likely never to return. The Native people had learned to adapt themselves to the material goods given to them by the white man. The clothing and blankets made the winter cold easier to bear. The guns and knives enabled them to provide food for the tribe and furs to trade. The alcohol made it easier for the white men to control the Native American survivors.

The English were different from the French in that they wanted not only the animals bearing furs but also the land on which the animals lived—land that the Natives shared with the animals, land where Natives had proved that coexistence was possible between man and beast. The English wanted the land, and the Natives could not understand this. They knew nothing of landownership and did not understand the concept.

As the English demanded more and more land, the Natives grew resentful. Some spoke of war. They reacted as any man or animal would react when cornered. They came out fighting.

In 1760, when the English took control of New France, which the English called Canada, they tried to maintain the friendship of the Natives so they would not join their enemies. Unfortunately, the English actions and attitudes spoke louder than their words. The majority of the English looked on the Natives as a menace and a hindrance to their westward expansion.

At the time of the English takeover, the Natives were told that the rivers would run red with rum and that the English king would send them many rifles and other gifts. They were told that a fine blanket could be had for only two beaver pelts. This pleased the Natives, and they welcomed the English to the Great Lakes region with open arms.

Because of the Seven Years' War the English were fighting in Europe, they failed to push into the Mississippi River region and take over the French posts there. England needed all its powder and other resources in Europe and saw little value in sending anything to North America to trade with the Natives or to help the English troops there to maintain control. Frenchmen still in the Mississippi River region supplied Native Americans with ammunition and powder and started many rumors about the English to arouse the Native war spirit.

When the British took control of the territory, the intense hatred left over from the war led to many disturbing incidents. At Fort St. Joseph (Niles), the Frenchman Louis Chevalier was accused of encouraging an attack by the Natives on the British troops.

In 1773, the British commander at Detroit refused to issue any license to traders, either British or French at Fort St. Joseph (Niles), until the Natives behaved and made an effort to follow the rules.

The Natives had always favored the French over the English. French trappers and traders very often married Native women and treated the Native men with respect. The French became expert woodsmen and took on many of the Native American ways of life.

By 1763, it had become apparent to the Natives that the English were very different from the French. The English did not fulfill their promises. The English looked down on the Natives and treated them as inferior. The rivers did not flow red with rum as promised, and it became difficult for the Natives to get the necessary supplies on which they had learned to depend. They became greatly dissatisfied and were willing to listen to the rumors spread by the French, who wanted to regain control of the fur trade. The Native American unhappiness soon grew into outright hatred of the English. Many plans and threats were made against the British, and the seeds for the "Conspiracy of Pontiac" were planted.

The English attitude of superiority was not limited to the Natives, but was directed at the colonists on the eastern seaboard as well. This attitude led not only to the British loss of the Great Lakes region but also to the eventual loss of the North American colonies.

During the "Conspiracy of Pontiac" in 1763, the British successfully defended Fort Pontchartrain (or Fort Detroit as it was then being called), but they lost control of Fort Michilimackinac to the Natives. It was a full year before they were able to regain control of that area. Fort St. Joseph at Niles was also lost during the Pontiac uprising.

Before 1763, the American colonies had been largely neglected by the British government. Left to their own devices, the people of the colonies became accustomed to managing their own affairs. As a result, when England decided to maintain garrisons in America and levy taxes to help defray the costs of their wars in Europe, there was strong opposition from the colonies.

Ignorant of the conditions in America and of the temperament of the colonists, the English Parliament repealed all taxes that offended the American colonies, retaining only a small tax on tea in order to demonstrate its authority. Resentment over this tax soon grew, and when ships bearing tea set anchor in Boston on December 16, 1773, a group of men, disguised as Native Americans, dumped chests of tea into Boston Harbor.

In 1774, Parliament retaliated by passing four new laws to reduce the political power of the people and closed the port of Boston. These laws were called the "Intolerable Acts." A fifth law, the Quebec Act, was passed that had no bearing on the colonies, but they regarded it as a threat to their liberties, in that it put an end to their claims on certain colonies to lands west of the Allegany Mountains.

The American colonists' revolt against the Stamp Act and the additional tax on tea started slow at first, soon building up steam and becoming widely supported. England now had more trouble on its hands than it realized. But as usual, it was slow to correctly read the situation. Due to the British indifference to the colonists and inhumane treatment of Native Americans, England was about to lose a major portion of its property in North America.

Michigan did not play a decisive role in the American Revolution, but Detroit was the base of operations for British raids into the Ohio and Kentucky regions. Detroit was also used as a prisoner of war camp and at one time had nearly five hundred captives. The British, fearing that Colonel George Rogers Clark, commander of Kentucky, could easily capture the vulnerable Fort Detroit, where it sat on the east bank of the Detroit River, decided to build a new fort farther back from the river. In 1779, Captain Richard B. Lernoult built Fort Lernoult on the property where the U.S. Federal Building in downtown Detroit now stands.

At Fort Michilimackinac, British Major Patrick Sinclair also feared an attack by Clark. Knowing that his Fort Michilimackinac was essentially indefensible and in need of major repairs, he built a new fort on Mackinac Island. This new fort, built on a bluff overlooking a natural harbor, was completed in 1781. He named it Fort Mackinac. It was thought to be virtually impregnable. The construction of Fort Mackinac turned out to be unnecessary, for Colonel Clark was unable to gather sufficient troops and provisions to attack Detroit, much less travel north to Fort Mackinac.

In 1780, Major Sinclair sent Charles Langlade and several hundred men to attack the Spaniards in St. Louis. Spain was not an ally of the United States, but it had declared war on England. Langlade's force was defeated and forced to quickly retreat back to Fort St. Joseph at Niles.

Fort St. Joseph at Niles was not garrisoned by the British after the "Conspiracy of Pontiac," but instead it became the headquarters for local French traders. When the French learned that a party of British troops was returning to the post, they left the fort quickly. They were soon overtaken by the British, and most were killed or captured. Those who were able to get away fled into the wilderness to live with their Native American friends.

When the Spanish in St. Louis learned of the British attack on the French traders, they felt the need to avenge the French victims. More than likely the Spaniards smelled a chance to get a foothold in the Michigan Territory. When two Milwaukee Native chiefs requested Spanish help to plunder the stores of Fort St. Joseph, the commander at St. Louis, Francisco Cruzat, gave his approval for the expedition to the Natives so that they would not discover Spain's weakness to defend itself directly. By allowing the expedition, Cruzat hoped to engender hostilities between the British and Natives loyal to the British, thereby causing them to become loyal to Spain. With great resolve, the Spanish sent an expedition from St. Louis to Fort St. Joseph. They arrived on February 12, 1781, but found it vacant. The British had already moved on. After raising the Spanish flag, they unexpectedly left the fort the next day and returned to St. Louis. Because of this Spanish action, Niles is known as the "City of Four Flags"—French, British, Spanish, and American, the only city in Michigan to claim this honor.

The Spanish march on Fort St. Joseph was caused by two aspects of Spanish policies. Spain's Native American policy was to use the Natives as a buffer between themselves and the American westward expansion and also to cause hostilities between the British and the Natives. With time, it may have worked.

The American Revolution, as we know, did not go well for the British and officially ended in 1783 with the signing of the Treaty of Paris. Due to either the negotiating skills of the American delegates or the clumsiness of the British delegates, the Michigan Territory was ceded to the United States. Historians are quite sure that the British king had no intention of giving up this land and that his negotiators did so completely without his authority.

Just twenty years after they had taken the land east of the Mississippi from the French, the British gave it to the Americans. The British people were glad to be rid of it. The garrisons were expensive to maintain, and settlers moving west had caused many problems. England, tired of the war with the Americans and willing to make concessions, retained only their western posts. But it was thirteen years before the United States was able to physically take control of the Michigan Territory. The reason for this seems to have been that the English king just did not want to give up the lucrative fur trade.

In 1796, the Jay Treaty was signed, ending British occupation of the western posts. On July 11, 1796, American troops arrived at Fort Lernoult at Detroit and raised the U.S. flag, taking formal possession of the Michigan Territory. In October, the British also withdrew from Fort Mackinac and moved to St. Joseph Island in upper Lake Huron just northeast of Mackinac Island. Finally, the Michigan Territory was completely under the control of the United States, or so it was thought. Legal title to the land meant little to the French and English traders still operating in the area.

The U.S. elections of 1810 brought to Congress a number of young men from the West and South, who came to be known as the "War Hawks." The War Hawks declared that it was the destiny of the United States to extend its territories to the North Pole. They boasted that Canada could be conquered in six weeks or less.

By 1812, after a long series of incidents on the sea arising out of the struggles between England and France, the United States had reached a point of breaking relations with Great Britain. The United States declared itself to be neutral concerning any and all things European. Both England and France disregarded the rights of neutral nations in their attempt to blockade each other. England had control of the sea, and its interference with neutral trade was very effective.

The combination of English and French interference with U.S. trade and the proclamation of northern expansion by the War Hawks ignited the war spirit of the young nation. The ongoing policy of England to stop American ships and force U.S. sailors to serve on British ships opened a wound that only a war could stop. On June 18, 1812, President James Madison signed a declaration of war against the British empire.

Communication between the eastern authorities and the Upper Lakes region was very poor. Somehow, within three weeks, the British commander at the fort on Canada's St. Joseph Island was informed of the declaration of war. On the morning of July 17, 1812, a British force of nearly one thousand troops and Native allies landed on the north side of Mackinac Island, at a spot now called "British Landing," and at sunrise had cannons pointed down at Fort Mackinac from the hilltop above the fort, forcing the American commander, Lieutenant Porter Hanks, to surrender the fort without firing a single shot. The British had moved into position on the hill overlooking the fort during the night. When the U.S. troops awoke that morning, they were staring up the barrels of English cannons.

On August 16, 1812, General Hull surrendered Fort Lernoult in Detroit to the British. At that time, the Michigan Territory once again effectively passed back into the hands of the British.

Britain held on to the Great Lakes region throughout the War of 1812 and was greatly surprised when it learned it had lost the war. Again the skills of the American negotiating team re-secured the Michigan Territory. The Treaty of Ghent was signed on December 24, 1814, ending the war and restoring the original international boundaries that existed before the war.

On July 18, 1815, the British again withdrew from Fort Mackinac. This time they moved to Drummond Island, where they built Fort Colyer, later to be known as Fort Drummond. A boundary survey in 1822 proved that Drummond Island actually belonged to the United States, and the British again had to move back to their old fort site on St. Joseph Island.

While on Drummond Island, the British built Fort Colyer and constructed barracks, dining halls, and a headquarters building, along with many stone fireplaces. A number of these fireplaces still exist on the island. Two of them are on private property, and a number of them still stand in the surrounding woods, which have grown up around and inside them.

The Ordinance of 1787, passed by the U.S. Continental Congress, provided a government for the Northwest Territory, which included Michigan. According to the ordinance, there were three stages in the progress of the territory toward statehood. First, there had to be a panel consisting of a governor, a secretary, and three judges appointed by the president. This was accomplished in Michigan very quickly.

The second stage required that the territory have five thousand free male inhabitants, which could then lead to the territory being separated from other territory.

The third stage would be reached when the territory had sixty-three thousand free white inhabitants. This number could not include any Native American population. At that point, the territory could then adopt a constitution and be admitted to the Union as a state equal in rights to the original thirteen states.

Michigan became a territory in 1805, and Lewis Cass was appointed by the president to be the first territorial governor in 1814. A fierce and bitter legislative battle with Ohio for the land referred to as the Toledo Strip began immediately. In a concessionary move, Ohio retained control of the Toledo Strip, and Michigan was given the Upper Peninsula. At the time, it was the opinion of most that Michigan got the short end of that legislative stick. The full extent of the natural resources in the Upper Peninsula was not known at the time. Only later did Michigan residents understand how valuable this piece of land would become. Rich in iron ore, copper, and white pine and at least one gold mine, the Upper Peninsula would eventually turn a number of far-sighted men into millionaires.

On January 26, 1837, Michigan was granted full statehood.

Part II

THE CONSPIRACY OF PONTIAC

When the English took control of New France (Canada) and the Great Lakes region in 1760, after 150 years of French domination, they wanted to maintain friendly relations with the Native Americans, just as the French had enjoyed. Holding council with the Natives, the English promised that they would be treated fairly and that trade would not be interrupted. The Natives were also promised that the rivers would flow red with rum and that the English king would send them many fine gifts.

In 1760, the English authorities decided that they needed all their gunpowder and other provisions for a war they were fighting in Europe. They could send very little to the colonies and trading posts in North America. After a century and a half of dependence on French trade goods, the Natives suddenly found themselves having to depend on British promises that were routinely broken. It was difficult for them to obtain the necessary goods for everyday life. They had forgotten how to provide their own clothing, had grown dependent on guns rather than bow and arrow, and had developed an insatiable desire for brandy and rum. The Natives found it very difficult, and some were unwilling to return to their old tribal lifestyles.

Early one morning in 1761, while the low-lying fog still clung to the tree branches, Chief Pontiac stood on a large outcropping of rock overlooking a small lake in what is today Oakland County, Michigan. He was holding the hand of his young daughter and spoke to his wife, Kantuckee Gun, saying, "What can we do? How do we stop them?"

Pontiac was referring to the British military, while trying to tamp down his hatred for them. "They take our land; they treat us with contempt and disrespect us like children; they kill our wild game disrupting our food supply; but worst of all they poison our people with their alcohol."

Typically in a Native American marriage, the wife had no public voice in the decision-making for the tribe. Quite possibly a wife or mother could influence how the children were raised, but overall decisions were often dominated by men. However, Pontiac and his wife, Kantuckee Gun, had a close and loving relationship, and it had been noticed by his people that Pontiac talked frequently with his wife about tribal plans. So it was no surprise to anyone when she told Pontiac that she objected to the plan to drive the English off their lands unless it also included the French. Her objection was due to her negative view of tribal men drinking so much alcohol and ruining their lives waiting for the English and the French to give them more whiskey or brandy. She wanted to run *all* the whites out, both the English and the French.

Kantuckee Gun said, "Yes, my husband. We see things happening, yet yours is the only voice speaking out against the British. I fear for your life if the British should take your words seriously."

"Many of my brothers take me seriously," Pontiac replied. "They too recognize the loss of our game animals and our hunting and camping grounds. But, no one seems to have any idea how we can drive the whites off our land so we can return to the traditions of our ancestors."

In a quiet voice, Kantuckee Gun said, "Last night, before sleep overtook you, you mentioned a war council."

"Yes," Pontiac replied. "A war council looks to be the only way to resolve this problem. My brothers and I will decide how to make war upon the British and to drive them from our land."

There are aspects of Pontiac's early life where some questions still linger. For his tribal affiliation, Chief Pontiac had always identified himself as Ottawa, although his mother was Chippewa and his father was Catawba. His wife, Kantuckee Gun, was a member of the Ottawa tribe, so it is believed that he chose her tribe to appease her. It is believed that he was born between 1712 and 1715. A number of tribal locations in the Upper Midwest have laid claim to his birth, with Pontiac Park at Defiance, Ohio, having the loudest voice.

Talks of war began to circulate through the tribes. By the summer of 1761, war belts were sent from one tribe to another, which was the method used when asking for help in a war. Chief Pontiac started gathering support from all the tribes in territories of Ohio, Indiana, Illinois, and Michigan.

The British began to hear rumors of war and decided to reinforce Fort Detroit, while leaving the smaller forts in the territory to fend for themselves.

In the spring of 1763, Chief Pontiac held a tribal council at Detroit, and many Natives from different tribes, along with a few Frenchmen, attended. Pontiac made a rousing speech, recalling to memory the kindness of the French and painting a clear picture in the minds of the Native American as to the wrongs that the English were doing to them. He excited his Native brothers by telling them that they were being neglected and lied to by the English. He told them that their French brothers would never do that.

Gradually, the Natives were worked into a fevered pitch, wanting only to drive the lying English from their land so their French friends could return. With that intention, the Conspiracy of Pontiac was born.

One significant trait of Chief Pontiac seems to be that he was a man of great dignity. He was not a rum-soaked chieftain, the likes of which would become familiar in the West a century later, but a leader of men who understood his own worth. Dignity was the one quality British dominance never tolerated among Native Americans. When it came down to it, the basic cause of the war we refer to as the Conspiracy of Pontiac was the fact that the British did not like the Native Americans and did not try to mask their contempt. That same inability to disguise their contempt for people whom they considered inferior led the British to their eventual loss of the American colonies.

Pontiac's only control over the other Native tribes was his natural ability of persuasion. In the hierarchy of the Native American tribes, there was no power given to an individual or formal group to decide what, if anything, would be done about the English. The power of a Native chief was more honorary than functional. Each tribe—or, for that matter, each man in the tribe—could decide for itself whether to make war or not. Pontiac's persuasive ability was the key that led to this violent portion of Michigan history.

The agreed-on plan was that on the first full moon of June, the local Native tribes would attack Forts Detroit, St. Joseph, Sandusky, and Michilimackinac. The plan for driving the English out of the Great Lakes region was decided. On the given day, the Natives, in their respective areas, would attack the English forts and kill all the troops. They had decided that total elimination of the English was the only way to achieve their goal.

The French were also busy with their plans to regain from the British what had been their exclusive territory in the fur trade. They went to great lengths conspiring to use the Native Americans to disrupt British life on the frontier.

After the British won their war against the French and took control of New France, they had promised all Native American tribes that no new forts would be built by the British. The ink was not even dry on that treaty when General Jeffrey Amherst, the architect of British policy toward Native Americans, ordered a new fort to be built on the southern shore of Lake Erie, called Fort Sandusky.

Amherst quickly went to work changing dozens of policies dealing with Native Americans. He cut back the practice of gift giving, which Amherst considered to be nothing more than bribes. Amherst then restricted the distribution of gunpowder and ammunition, along with other supplies that the Native Americans used for hunting. By that time, many Natives had long since forgotten most of the old ways for hunting, trapping, and clothing themselves. Amherst raised the number of beaver pelts required from the Natives in order to get the items on which they had become dependent.

The Natives knew that they were being taken advantage of and also that many of their people were caving to the power of rum and brandy, which the British used as a way to control the local tribes. Many tribal leaders saw this destruction. The Natives began to get restless.

Early in 1761, some tribal leaders began calling for tribes to join together to drive the British out and to bring the French back in. A Native American prophet named Neolin called for Native American tribes to reject all European control and to return to traditional Native ways. This was something that Pontiac agreed with.

During the years before Pontiac's War, a British officer, Robert Rogers, claimed to have met with Pontiac and discussed what the Native Americans actually wanted from the British. According to Rogers, Pontiac's response was quick and to the point: "Leave now or we shall rise up and kill all of you in one swift motion." In 1761, when Rogers published his account of the meeting, he made Chief Pontiac the most famous Native American of the eighteenth century. It did more than that—it actually began the process of mythologizing him.

Fort St. Joseph had started out as a mission and trading post built by the French Jesuits on the banks of the St. Joseph River near present-day Niles. The land had originally been given to the Jesuits in 1684 by the French king in order to build a mission and trading post. In 1691, a French military commander built a military post next to the mission in an effort to protect the profitable fur trade. The fort was fairly small, with only fifteen houses in and around the fort that could accommodate about thirty soldiers, along with the Jesuits.

On May 25, 1763, unwilling to wait for the full moon of June, a war party of Potawatomi Natives attacked Fort St. Joseph at Niles and killed the entire garrison except for four men. These four men were later taken to Detroit and exchanged for some of the goods the English had promised.

Fort Michilimackinac, built in 1715, became a fully manned fort after the British took control of the territory. There were still a few French fur traders sneaking through to trade with the Natives, but there was no real trouble caused by this so the British allowed it to continue. Michilimackinac had ninety-three British military men assigned to the fort, with a group of eight officers along with the fort commander, Captain Richard Etherington. There were also a few British families and French families living outside the walls of the fort.

On a beautiful day in early June, the Native American tribe living near the fort decided to play their tribal game (similar to lacrosse) in the open space outside the fort walls near the main gate. The British were in a festive mood celebrating the king's birthday and welcomed the distraction.

Native American women holding long blankets were standing against the outside of the fort wall near the gate. The game went back and forth between the goals until, all of a sudden, the ball was hit over the wall and into the fort. The guards opened the gates, and the Native players rushed into the fort to retrieve the ball as if still playing the game. Grabbing weapons from under the blankets of the Native women, the Native players proceeded to kill more than half the British soldiers. Captain Etherington and the remaining soldiers were released after weeks of torture.

Weeks before, Captain Etherington had been warned of the possibility of being attacked, but he paid little attention. The Natives had been behaving in a friendly manner for weeks, so he gave the caution no further consideration.

The Natives gained control of the fort, took all the goods they wanted, and then burned the fort to the ground. It was a full year before the English were able to return and secure the area.

The attack on Fort Pontchartrain was led by Chief Pontiac and, ironically, was the only attack that was not successful. Pontiac gained entry into the fort by requesting a council with Major Gladwin. Pontiac and his party of sixty warriors entered the fort and were greeted by a stern but friendly Gladwin, who had his soldiers on duty and prepared for hostility.

Pontiac's plan was to sit down with Gladwin to discuss local trade policy. He would then rise, make a speech, and then present Gladwin with a wampum belt in a certain manner that had been prearranged to signal the attack. The Natives in the fort had hidden guns under their blankets. When it came time to present the wampum belt, there was a drumroll. A door to the council was opened, and there stood a group of British soldiers ready for the attack. One of the soldiers pulled back the blanket of a Native woman to expose a hidden gun. The Natives were taken by surprise. The attack on Fort Pontchartrain was thwarted.

Pontiac, who was totally surprised but diplomatic enough, finished his speech and then presented the wampum belt, but not in the prearranged manner. Major Gladwin rose and spoke to the group of Natives. He told them the English would be friends with them as long as they remained peaceful. If they wanted a war, he would not hesitate to show them the full power of the English king.

How Gladwin learned of the attack has never been fully explained. He did not record the matter in his personal papers, possibly to protect the identity and life of the informant should the Natives seek revenge. One theory is that Gladwin had been informed by a Native maiden who came to sell him a pair of moccasins. Another story suggests that a group of Frenchmen loyal to the English gave a warning of the attack. Still another story says that the daughter of M. Cuillerier, a French trader who was planning the attack with Pontiac, overheard the plans. She was in love with a Scottish trader living at the fort and possibly told him of the plans in order to save his life.

The day after the thwarted attack, Pontiac and a group of warriors showed up at the fort and said that they wanted to smoke the peace pipe with Major Gladwin. The commander told Pontiac that he and a few chieftains could enter after he was searched, but the rest of the Natives had to stay outside. This angered Pontiac, and he no longer tried to keep the false face of peace.

During the summer of 1763, from May to October, the Natives were directed by Chief Pontiac to lay siege to Fort Pontchartrain. A siege of this duration had never been known in Native American history. More than one hundred English traders and settlers living outside the walls of the fort were killed by the warring Natives.

On June 30, a fleet of canoes coming upriver was spotted by a fort sentry. A cheer went up. All wondered if the Natives would attack the canoes. The Englishmen in the canoes did not return the customary salute from the fort. Suddenly, a Native war whoop was heard. The Englishmen in the canoes had been taken prisoner on Lake Erie by Chief Pontiac's tribe. Twenty-six canoes of provisions floated past the fort and landed at the Native village.

One of the cruelest incidents in Michigan history followed. One by one, the Englishmen from the canoes were tortured beyond human endurance. The sounds of the anguished screams lasted for hours, far into the night.

Then their bodies were thrown into the river to float past the fort, where they could be seen by the soldiers. The English were appalled and frightened.

On July 29, English Captain Dalzell, along with 280 men and supplies, reached the fort under cover of a heavy fog. The renewed hope brought by Captain Dalzell was short-lived. Gladwin gave Dalzell permission to attack the Indians, but Dalzell was not an experienced fighter and greatly underestimated the strength of the Native American force. The English attack was a disaster.

In October, Pontiac received word from Fort Chartres, the French fort in the Illinois Territory, that the French would no longer give him aid because the French had negotiated a peace treaty with the English. Pontiac then began to realize that he was being used by the French. Defeated and humiliated, Pontiac left the Great Lakes area. He had planned to return the next summer and take up the siege again, but he did not do so. After the Natives broke the siege in October and returned to the winter hunting grounds, it was nearly impossible to gather them together again. When Pontiac did return to Michigan, he asked for peace.

On April 20, 1769, in a Native village near Cahokia, Ohio, Chief Pontiac was assassinated by a Native American man who was avenging his uncle, whom Pontiac had fatally stabbed during a disagreement three years earlier. After further investigation, it was found that a Peoria Native American tribal council had authorized Pontiac's execution. The execution was carried out not just because Pontiac had stabbed and killed the man but also because it was determined that Chief Pontiac was becoming a larger problem for the tribes due to his constant skirmishes with British military troops. The Native American tribal leadership in Ohio and Michigan had accepted that the whites were taking over the land and that there was nothing they could do about it. So the decision was made that Chief Pontiac had to go.

Many rumors have developed and many stories have been told about the circumstances of Pontiac's death, which included different British operatives handling and mishandling the assassination, but there is no actual testimony or evidence to support these stories.

Chief Pontiac's actual burial place is not known. There are stories that his body was moved and buried in St. Louis. In 1900, the Daughters of the American Revolution placed a plaque on the southeast corner of Walnut and South Broadway in St. Louis, which was claimed to be near the burial place.

Another story holds that Chief Pontiac's body was moved and buried on Apple Island in Orchard Lake, a lake that lies within Oakland County,

Michigan. The Apple Island burial has not yet been proven and may never be, but many believe that this location makes the most sense given his strong ties to the local tribes.

At this point in Michigan history, the final resting place of Chief Pontiac is unknown.

Part III

FORT CONSTRUCTION

Military forts have played an important role in American history from the moment the Spanish, French, and English trappers/traders and military units landed in North America. One of the first things that their military units did was build forts for protection—protection for the trappers and for the land that the militaries claimed for their king.

Forts existed in the American colonies and throughout North America in the seventeenth and eighteenth centuries to defend trappers and traders from Native American attacks, and they became critical pieces in the continental chess match European countries played against one another for control of the North American continent. Unfortunately, the group most affected by the often shameful acts of the Europeans were the Native Americans.

When the Revolutionary War broke out in 1775 between the British empire and the American colonists, many of the forts immediately became important military targets.

There are three basic considerations that should be kept in mind when studying frontier fortifications. First was the public concern, whether it was French, British, or American, for limiting the expense of frontier forts. Secondly, these frontier forts were designed principally to house and provide for the movement of stores and supplies. Finally, they had to be defendable by a small number of troops.

Forts were always positioned in important locations or constructed at strategic points on the landscape so the trapping and trade interests could be protected. These locations were often where waterways or roads converged. The forts were built to defend these travel ways and also protect Native American trading partners.

At the start of the Revolutionary War, the North American continent was already dotted with forts that had been constructed even before the French and Indian War, which had started in 1754. Among these forts were large masonry forts like Fort Ticonderoga, which is in upstate New York. It was manned by a small force of British soldiers when the Revolutionary War broke out in 1775. On May 10, 1775, Benedict Arnold and Ethan Allen captured the fort and all its military personnel without firing a shot. During that winter, American Colonel Henry Knox moved the artillery from Ticonderoga to Cambridge, Massachusetts, which proved to be decisive in driving the British from Boston in 1776.

Early in the war, forts were quickly constructed where they would be needed to protect armies. One of the most important fortified positions in North America was at West Point, New York, which is now the U.S. Army Military Academy. It was often described as "the key to the continent." In 1780, American General Benedict Arnold betrayed the United States and conspired with the British to capture West Point. The plot ultimately failed, but it showed the importance of the position of the West Point fortification on the New York Hudson River.

To build these forts and fortifications, armies used engineers to design the layout and construction using the latest military science and strategies. When the Revolutionary War broke out, there were very few Americans who had the engineering education and military understanding of how to construct a solid fortification.

The French were well known for their skill in designing forts, and both the British and Americans used their methods in designing and building somewhat modified fortifications. The American Continental army enlisted Polish engineer Thaddeus Kosciuszko to help with the construction of forts. Kosciuszko played an important role in building American fortifications at battlefields across the continent during the war. In addition to fortifying important locations, Kosciuszko traveled with the Continental army and personally helped with building forts on-site, even during major battles.

There is a large statue of General Thaddeus Kosciuszko, astride his horse, standing in downtown Detroit.

IT QUICKLY BECAME APPARENT to American commanders that the tactics of battlefield warfare in the eighteenth century dictated that forts were important and decisive components of warfare. Many of the same tactics and fortifications would continue to be used by military commanders even during the American Civil War. In some cases, such as at Yorktown, the earthworks used by the Revolutionary War soldiers were also used by Civil War soldiers almost one hundred years later, displaying the universal importance of forts and fortifications in military history.

The construction of a fortification is as old as human conflict, and secure defensive positions have often played an important part in warfare. Their design and construction have changed steadily, always in response to the weaponry brought against them, whether stones, arrows, cannons, or aircraft, as in more recent wars.

The eighteenth century was a time of intensive military activity in Europe and in the Americas. The period from the 1680s to the French Revolution in the 1780s has been called the "classic century of military engineering," a time when earlier forms of artillery fortifications were perfected and frequently tested in battle.

Designing, constructing, and recording fortifications was the job of the military engineer. They trained themselves to follow well-tested principles of design, based on geometry, to construct fortified places. These principles were recorded in detailed plans, many of surprising complexity, but most early period forts in North America were of a simple square box design with redoubts built on opposite corners.

The armament of potential attackers influenced the design of a fortification. Fort Franklin was a U.S. post situated on the overland route from Pittsburgh to Erie, Pennsylvania. Native Americans were the most likely threat to the area, but the proximity of Lake Erie meant possible attack from British troops from Canada. Fort Franklin was therefore constructed of horizontal logs to better resist light artillery.

An eighteenth-century fort relied heavily on bastions for support. Bastions are angular projections from the walls that provide stable platforms for the defenders and their weaponry. Bastions were placed at corners of a fortified enclosure and laid out so that the fire of the defenders could cover all parts of the walls and adjacent bastions to prevent attackers from finding any kind of shelter. Full bastions consisted of two sides and two faces that, with the side open to the fort, formed a pentagonal structure. The number and design of bastions varied according to the shape and size of the enclosure to be protected. Most forts had between two and five.

The engineer would determine the exact position and shape of each bastion using geometrical calculations suggested by Sébastien Le Prestre Vauban. It was critical that the structure be placed so as to allow effective flanking fire. Vauban's treatise included explanations of the different types of angles found in a fortification and a glossary of the bewildering variety of measurements used in different European nations and their American territories.

The European colonizers of North America brought familiar styles of fortification from their home countries. Initially, Native Americans were the most likely threat on land as they resisted the invasion of their territories. The invasion of North America by the Europeans led to the eventual nearly complete destruction of Native American tribes. By drawing the Native Americans into the fur trading treaties using useful items, along with alcohol, the Europeans were able to control and eliminate many Native cultures.

A square stockade with bastions or blockhouses on opposite corners was more economical for the number of fort defenders that would be needed. The fortifications provided quarters for officers and enlisted men, along with wives. Outside the walls of the fort, there was usually space for small gardens.

The choice of a site for a fortification was influenced by strategic and tactical considerations. In eighteenth-century North America, the strategic concerns were often related to transportation routes made up of lakes and rivers and some inland trails. Portages between water systems were particularly vulnerable, as were the rudimentary roads cut by military forces at inland locations.

The strategic site for a fortification was the responsibility of a senior military commander, who best knew how fortified bases would support the operations of his command. A good example of this would be when British Colonel Patrick Sinclair ordered Fort Mackinac to be built on the island and then moved his entire British garrison to the new island fort; the abandoned Fort Michilimackinac was left to rot and eventually covered over by sand.

All military fortifications built on Michigan soil were built of timber-frame design, with only one exception. Fort Mackinac, built on a bluff 150 feet above the harbor on Mackinac Island, was built out of limestone. As a testament to that construction, Fort Mackinac is the only military fortification built on Michigan soil prior to 1837 that is still standing.

Once a decision had been made regarding the need for a fort, it was up to the engineer to determine the type of construction that would best achieve the goals of the commander. An engineer or another officer with cartographic skills was responsible for preparing a map showing the location to be defended or the topography that influenced the placement and design of the fort.

Sometimes the need for a fortification to protect a town or harbor made it necessary to compromise its defense by placing it close to commanding ground, as was the case with Fort Mackinac. Later, during the American

Revolution, it quickly became apparent to the American commander of Fort Mackinac that the high hilltop above Fort Mackinac left his garrison completely defenseless against attack from that location.

The process of designing a fort was influenced by many factors. These include the strategic and tactical reasons for occupying the position, the topography within which the fortification was placed, the nature of the weapons that an enemy might direct against it, and the presence of existing structures that could be removed or incorporated.

For regular fortifications, historical memory would recommend designing a fort from the exterior. That is, the engineer established the location of the salient points (the tips) of the bastions and from the geometrically established lines that placed the flanks and faces of the bastions and the curtain walls that connected them.

It was seldom possible to design a perfectly regular fortification. Engineers were expected to take the topography of the site into consideration, which meant designing and building the fortification to conform to the land on which it was built.

Transferring a plan from paper to the actual ground was the next step in constructing a fortification. Using a compass and sighting arm, the engineer would then determine a line through the center of each projected bastion. The work crew would measure the distance to the salient (tip) of each bastion and place a stake at that point. They would move the plane to the salient and then permit the rest of the fort's outline to be measured and marked so construction could begin.

The fortifications of eighteenth-century America were constructed of a variety of materials. Major works were built of packed earth faced with stone or brick. The earthen walls of some less complex artillery forts, such as Niagara, were faced with sod to slow erosion. These were expensive and time-consuming forms of construction. Wood was a more economical though biodegradable building material, and it was practical because most North American fortifications were not expected to be permanent. They were constructed in haste because of the proximity of an enemy, and the ready supply of timber had only to be removed from the forest.

Timber was used for two primary types of fort construction. Log works were built of two parallel horizontal log walls separated by the intended thickness of the finished barrier. The void between them was filled with earth or rubble excavated from the ditch that was dug surrounding the fort.

The other form of log construction was the picketed fort or stockade. Logs, usually of about fifteen feet in length and pointed at one end, were placed vertically in a three-foot-deep trench that followed the lines of the fort. Stockades could not stand against cannon fire, and they soon rotted at ground level (the usual "lifetime" of a stockade picket was eight to ten years), but they were effective against attackers who lacked cannons and they were easy to construct in frontier areas.

Permanent fortifications required barracks, officers' quarters, and various types of storehouses to shelter and support their garrisons. Plans of individual buildings are rare, but some were produced for reporting purposes or to obtain construction approval from superior officers.

Detailed floor plans identify interior features such as fireplaces, partitions, stairways, and even bunks for the soldiers. The difference in status between officers and enlisted men is neatly expressed by the amount of space allocated to each rank.

In the course of active campaigning, military forces were often in need of simplified fortifications that could be constructed rapidly and did not require complicated designs or plans. Fieldworks usually lacked bastions and simply comprised a ditch and wall surrounded by an abatis, an obstruction of fallen trees with their branches intertwined to impede an attacker. Fieldworks might stand alone or form a part of lines of defense around camps.

When U.S. General Anthony Wayne led his "Legionnaires" against the Native Americans of the Old Northwest in 1794, he ordered his men to refortify the army's camp each night. This is known because a British spy mapped the occupied camp each night prior to the American victory at Fallen Timbers. The British spy was discovered and his notes confiscated.

Fortifications on the eastern American frontier, up into what has been referred to as the Upper Midwest, have long been a subject of interest to local historians, whose knowledge and understanding of military architecture was limited to whatever local sources and traditions were apparent for a particular fort site.

European fort builders of the fifteenth century were faced with the introduction of gunpowder into warfare. This technological advance forever changed the character of fortification design. On the American frontier, few fortifications reached the sophistication of these European models.

Another vital concept for what the eighteenth-century military termed as "fieldworks," a contemporary term for what we today would call frontier forts, was put forward by a French engineer named Clairac, who wrote a volume titled *The Field Engineer*, which was translated and published in Philadelphia in 1776. George Washington had a copy of this work in his own personal library. The concept stated that a soldier defending a fort generally fires mechanically straight ahead rather than to the right or left.

Following the tenets of *The Field Engineer*, Clairac's concept of "lines of fire" and the components of the bastioned system itself did not dictate any single form for frontier fortifications. The outline of the French Fort Duquesne can be viewed as the "typical" bastioned fort in the frontier. A variation on that trace was the "half-bastion" or "demi-bastion," shown in the plat of Fort Lernoult, built by the British at Detroit in 1778. Henry Bird, the engineer for this fort, acknowledged that this trace was less perfect than full bastions. But the open configuration of half-bastions allowed for increased storage space on the interior. More importantly, the reduced number of faces and flanks on the bastions made them simpler and quicker to construct and thus less expensive.

The star trace used by the British to build Fort Bull in western New York in 1755 departed even more from the bastioned system by omitting corner emplacements entirely. The star-shaped design left many areas outside the fort uncovered, but according to one British military engineer in the 1780s, it was a popular form with Americans at the start of the Revolution, especially since it supposedly was invented by and remained a favorite of the French, who assumed the role of military tutors for the new American republic.

Military engineers considered the triangular form even less desirable, since it left uncovered with any field of fire significant segments of the area outside the fort. Still it was useful in situations where there were very small garrisons and a shortage of time or money to build a more sophisticated structure.

Civilian fortifications, particularly blockhouses, became the norm on the Old Northwest frontier during the War of 1812 because by this time there were a number of substantial areas of settlement even in the Upper Midwest. There are many contemporary drawings of blockhouses, both military and civilian, that describe two-story wooden structures with the second story projecting over the first. A number of these early nineteenth-century military structures are still standing in the northern United States.

A masonry first story for blockhouses was actually not rare on the frontier and was, in fact, recommended by some British military officers to increase the durability of a blockhouse and again reduce its long-term expense.

We can see how the basic fortification concepts developed in Europe were adapted in the American frontier. But if we take this a step further, a close examination of one particular structural element will give us an appreciation of the design choices available to the military engineer in the late eighteenth and early nineteenth centuries in North America.

The most basic architectural element of a frontier fort was its wall, and there was a great variety of construction techniques. By far the most common fort wall was the stockade. Contemporary accounts of frontier fort construction are replete with descriptions of this type of fortification. It was ideally suited to the capabilities of a nonmilitary force, requiring no special skills beyond an adeptness with an axe and shovel. While it provided a certain sense of security, a single-wall stockade was a flawed system. In the first place, a single row of logs with one end stuck in the ground produced a highly unstable structure, even with the standard rib band or strip of wood connecting each picket, so that it constantly required attention to provide any defense at all. Secondly, unless great care was taken in selecting the logs and placing them in the trench, there were frequently significant gaps between each log.

Military officers, therefore, insisted on either "lining" the walls with boards to cover the gaps or adding a second row of smaller pickets inside the first row, positioned between the outer rows to cover the gaps. By the early nineteenth century, this latter method had become the standard in the fortification classes taught by the Military Academy at West Point.

THE FRENCH FORT MAUREPAS from the late seventeenth century in the lower Mississippi Valley was clearly built by an insecure colonial power to guard against the incursions of the British. The walls in this case were constructed by the French commandant as a double row of large logs supplemented by a smaller row to the rear. In other words, it was a triple stockade intended to defend against light artillery.

An interesting variation to increase the stability of the stockade was designed by British engineers at Fort George in 1799, where every fourteenth picket was planted several feet farther into the ground than the adjacent pickets and was strengthened with a brace of horizontal and diagonal members at its base.

Another simpler variation on the "standard" stockade wall was used in Fort Necessity, Pennsylvania, constructed by Virginia militia under the direction of George Washington in 1754. The walls of Washington's odd little circular fort were composed of oak logs split in half with smaller posts on the interior to serve as musket rests or to simply fill gaps in the wall. The archaeologist who discovered this design for the National Park Service in the 1930s speculated that this wall may have been unique to Washington and a result of time and personnel shortages during its construction in the reduction of the quantity of trees that had to be felled. It should be noted, however, that this same wall design was still being used in the southern states eighty years later, so this technique may represent a regional characteristic of American origin.

Vertical stockade walls could also be combined with traditional horizontal log wall building construction to form the outer wall of the fortification.

Perhaps the simplest of all frontier fort walls were those erected by the U.S. Army and Kentucky militia in the Ohio Valley during the 1790s. These "temporary fortifications" were formed by cutting down trees to form a five-foot-high breastwork that was referred to as a "brush fence." Occasionally, where timber was scarce, the walls were formed of packed earth, and sometimes they needed to be re-packed on a daily basis to protect against a surprise attack.

All of the wall systems were only a defense against the limited armament of Indians and not a European enemy equipped with artillery. To defend against the latter type of attack required a more sophisticated structure intended to absorb the shock of artillery.

Most horizontal log walls were actually composed of two parallel walls tied together with a cross member to form a cribwork and then filled with earth. This system could be used by itself to form the walls of a fort. The technique were intended as a defense against artillery, but since it relied predominantly on wooden forms the forts were still susceptible to artillery. As a consequence, when the enemy was a European one, earthen walls were preferred.

During the eighteenth century, a clear distinction was made by military theorists between regular and irregular fortifications. Regular fortifications technically referred to a work whose defensive structures were all symmetrical and had equal components. There is evidence to suggest, however, that the term had an additional meaning to military officers in America. Anthony Wayne, for example, referred to a regular fortification as one defensible against artillery.

To construct an earthen wall fort, a wooden framework was prepared under the direction of the engineer. It served no structural function, but rather simply marked the limits of the parapet as a guide for workmen. The dirt for the outer ditch was then dug out and thrown into the framework. As

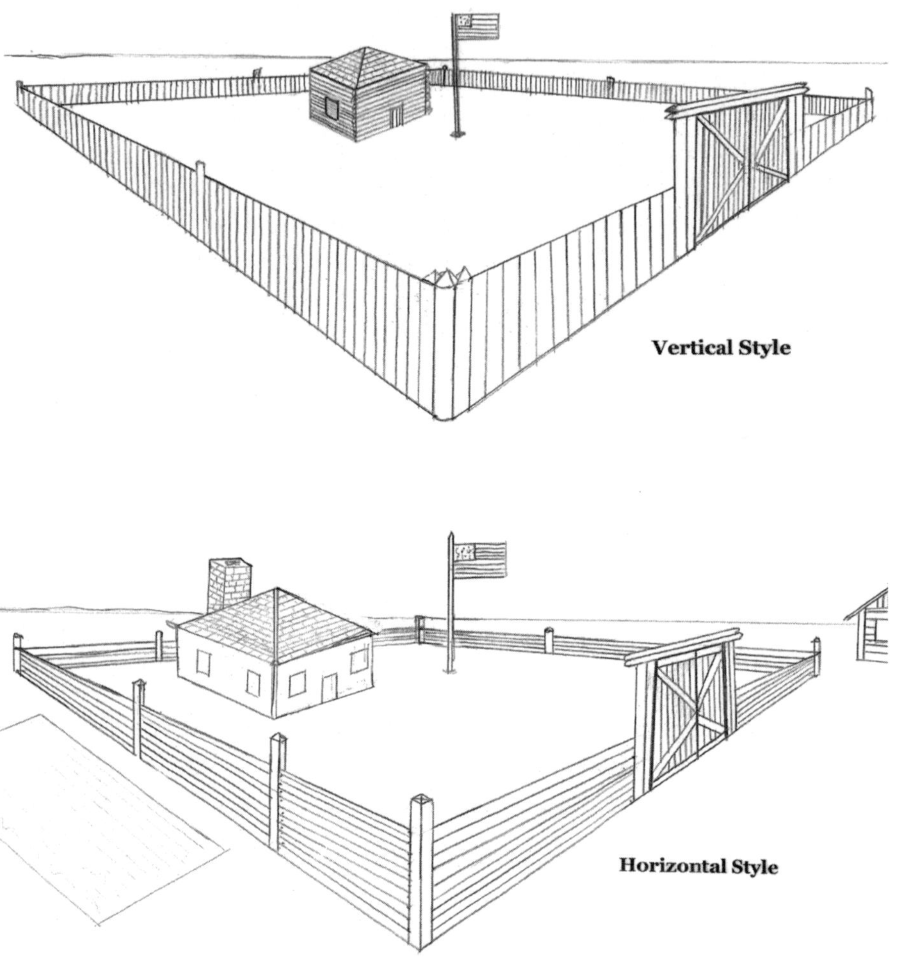

Vertical and horizontal log fort constructions. *Courtesy of author.*

the U.S. Military Academy at West Point developed its programs, officers were trained to calculate the time involved in erecting such a structure by determining how far an individual could throw the earth and at what rate, depending on the size of the final wall desired.

The dirt dug out of the trenches was unstable by itself and required some physical support to maintain its shape. Sod, cut in slabs and laid like brick, was one method of providing stability; in another method, the earth was secured with fascines (bundles of sticks), hurdles (a type of interwoven basket weave frame), gabions (woven baskets filled with earth), a scrap revetment formed of dovetailed planks, or heavy timber or stone slabs like at Fort Wayne in Detroit. All designs were covered in detail for officers at the U.S. Military Academy in the early nineteenth century.

What can we actually learn from the study of frontier fort construction? Too often the concept of frontier fortifications has been oversimplified by historians, with assumptions made that one fort was pretty much like another. But a whole host of various plans, materials, techniques, and functions governed seventeenth-, eighteenth-, and nineteenth-century fort design decisions.

The field of study of the military fortification structure is still a largely unexplored and promising area for future historians.

MICHIGAN FORTS

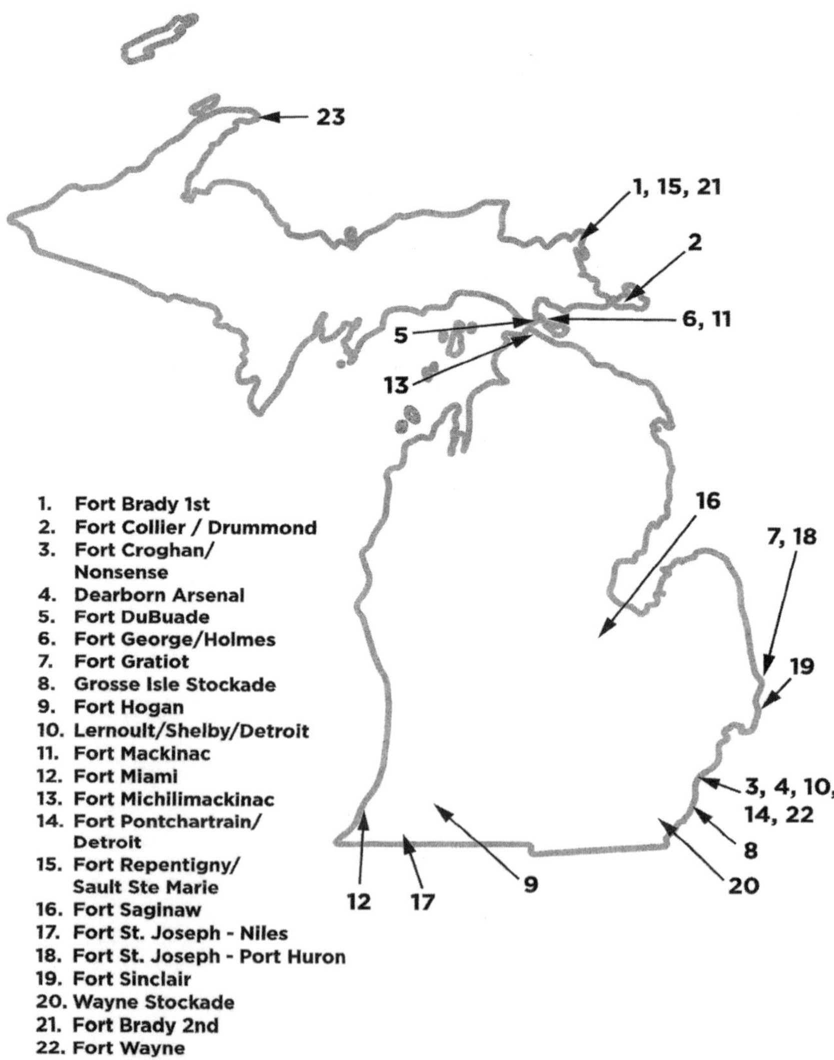

Michigan state map. *Courtesy of author.*

Part IV

FORTS BUILT BEFORE 1837

Fort Brady 1st

Sault Ste. Marie
1822–1893

In 1668, a French Jesuit mission was established at the location where Lake Superior dumps its water over a series of rapids to the lower elevation of the St. Mary's River. This first Jesuit mission lasted only two years. The Jesuits had intended to minister to the spiritual needs of the Native American tribes. They did not know or understand that the Native tribes would follow the seasonal movements of the game animals for their sustenance. When the local Chippewas left the area around the rapids, the Jesuits misread that to mean they were left with no one to minister to. In the year 1669, the Jesuits abandoned the mission. The next year, the French fur traders set up their business when small groups of local tribes returned to the abandoned mission, and soon furs of all kinds began to flow through the trading post to find their way to the European markets. It would be a number of years before the Jesuits would return to their old mission.

By this time, the Upper Midwest fur trade was developing into a business that caught the attention of the European markets along with the royal households. French fur trappers/traders operated throughout the area with little or no governmental restrictions, control, or protection. The old Jesuit mission site was used extensively by the French traders to provide furs of all kinds to the markets back in France. To provide protection for this lucrative trade, the French King Louis XV ordered that a fortified military structure be built at what would become Sault Ste. Marie to protect the fur trading interests of the French.

In 1750, Louis le Gardeur de Repentigny and Captain Louis de Bonne arrived at the old Jesuit mission and found the trading post in complete disarray. On the orders of the French king, De Repentigny directed his French soldiers in the construction of a military post and fortified it with two cannons. Per the king's orders, the fort was to be operated and maintained by De Repentigny, although he was frequently absent while traveling and exploring around lower Canada, leaving his employee/tenant Jean Baptiste Cadotte in charge of the day-to-day operations of the fort, including the fur trade. It was known, but not widely talked about, that De Repentigny kept a Native wife and more than one mixed child on tribal grounds northwest of present-day Brimley. This little family kept Captain Repentigny away from his military duties at the fort/mission/trading post that bore his name.

When De Repentigny and De Bonne planted the French flag in the soil at "the Sault," they were instructed by the king to lay claim to 214,000 acres of surrounding land, which the Native Americans called "Bowating." With that order issued in 1750, the king of France set the stage for a legal dispute that would not be settled until after the American Civil War.

As a result of the French and Indian War, the British acquired Canada and the Upper Midwest and took control of the old Jesuit mission and trading post in 1761. De Repentigny had been absent for a number of years, with Cadotte left in complete charge of the post. In 1762, during another period when De Repentigny was absent, a British force invaded the Upper Midwest Territory and took over a number of trading posts. When the British reached Fort Repentigny and attacked, Cadotte tried to defend the post but was severely undermanned and outgunned. The British took control of the post and the fur trade. The next year, on a dark and foggy night, fires broke out in every post building except the house conveniently owned by Cadotte. The fort and trading post were destroyed, but the British continued to occupy the site for a number of years in order to control the trading for furs with the Native tribes.

After the American Revolution and the 1783 Treaty of Paris, there were many disputes between the United States and Great Britain concerning the boundary lines of the Great Lakes. Originally, the Upper Peninsula was of no use or of any interest to the Americans, so there weren't many concerns over its boundaries until the War of 1812. Disputes began over the location of the border within the St. Mary's River, which covered sixty miles of waterway. With those disputes, the War of 1812 finally reached the fleets and armies stationed from Sault Ste. Marie all the way to Mackinac Island.

On December 24, 1814, President James Madison's negotiators reached a formal agreement for a determination of the boundaries of the Great Lakes. In the summer of 1815, the British formally surrendered Fort Mackinac, Fort Colyer on Drummond Island, and the old French Jesuit mission site used by fur traders to the Americans. The United States now had command of the entrance and exits of the St. Mary's River system.

Still, the British sought to maintain their control over the fur trade using their well-established relationship with the local Native American tribes around the Upper Great Lakes area. The Natives were by this time completely dependent on the trade goods provided by the British and saw no reason to welcome American rule. The Natives chose to continue their allegiance to Great Britain.

In 1815, the Americans decided to exert their authority and establish effective control over the Native tribes in the region. Garrisons were established at the key locations of Green Bay, Rock Island, Prairie du Chien, and at Sault Ste. Marie at the rapids. But by way of the Treaty of 1815, all the former Chippewa lands were returned to the tribes by the Americans. New negotiations were needed in order to rightfully build on Native land, so the U.S. government sent Lewis Cass, governor of the Michigan territory. Cass arrived in 1820 and explained the intention of the U.S. government to build a fortified military structure and the reasons why the fort was necessary.

After Cass finished with the explanation, many Natives were angered that the British would not step in to fix the situation. One angry man, Sassaba, brother of Chief Shingabowassin, pulled out a British flag and planted the flag in the ground at feet of Governor Cass. The governor knocked the flag down and stomped it into the dirt, declaring that the U.S. government could and would destroy their village.

The chief then summoned Susan Johnson, wife of legendary fur trader Joseph Johnson and sister to Sassaba, to calm her brother down. Bloodshed was avoided that day. At a Native council meeting a few weeks later, on June 16, 1820, sixteen square miles were ceded, by treaty, over to the American government, which included the twenty-six acres of land surrounding the old French fort.

In July 1822, U.S. Colonel Hugh Brady arrived with six companies of infantry and began the process and work of rebuilding a fortified military structure on the site of the old French Fort Repentigny. The outer structure was built using vertical timbers to enclose an area of nearly ten acres, which included log structures for the headquarters, officers' quarters, and single-story barracks for enlisted men.

A stockade of whitewashed cedar posts enclosed the fort. Blockhouses were built on opposing corners of the rectangular stockade, with sentry boxes built into each corner. Munition storage houses were built near the center. Horse stables and barns were built on the riverbank. The garrison field and cemetery were located south of the fort entrance, near where the old Federal building stands today. (Archaeologists have found buried evidence of three of the original walls.)

Private homes and gardens were established outside the walls of the fort. Life at the fort became routine and pleasurable for most men and their families. The Native tribes moved away from the fort but stayed in the area.

Fort Brady 1st was part of the northern frontier fortification of the United States. Colonel Brady needed and wanted an impressive display of power to confirm the power and assertion of American authority over the region.

Fort Brady was intended to be armed with ten eighteen-pounder cannons, five twelve-pounders, three field cannons, eight flank howitzers, two eight-inch heavy seacoast howitzers, two light ten-inch mortars, and five heavy mortars for a total of thirty-five heavy guns.

Originally, the military structure was known as Post at Sault Ste. Marie (1822), then Post at St. Mary's (1823–24), and then Cantonment Brady (1824–25). The post was abandoned in 1857 when the garrison was moved to Minnesota. Fort Brady was then re-garrisoned in 1866.

In 1838, the U.S. government, after receiving Congressional approval, was interested in digging out portions of the St. Mary's River rapids in order to build the Wenzel Lock and Canal. In May 1839, a contractor arrived with a gang of men to start the lock excavation. He had been warned by the fort commander not to interfere with the millrace for the fort sawmill. The contractor ignored the warning and did endanger the millrace. When he refused to stop, the fort commander used an army detachment to forcibly remove the workmen from the river.

In August 1838, the U.S. War Department and the Army Corps of Engineers reached an agreement with Michigan officials on the route and methods to be used. The original contractor refused to follow those directions and walked away, and the project was abandoned for a short time.

Portions of the old fort property were sold off starting in 1852, with the remaining portions of old Fort Brady and Fort Repentigny sold in 1893. The west stockade wall still exists as a part of an exhibit along the Historic Locks Park Walkway in Brady Park. Some of the former officers' quarters still exist, as they were incorporated into private homes.

In 1893, a new fort, Fort Brady 2nd, was built on the hill overlooking the St. Mary's River—a site chosen by General Phil Sheridan. After the U.S. removal of the garrison to the new fort in 1892–93, the old fort grounds were platted by Assistant Quartermaster George S. Hoyt. The growing city quickly covered over the remains of the old Fort Brady. Grave sites in the old fort cemetery were exhumed, and remains were reburied at another location.

In 1825, the DeBonne descendants began to press their claims to what had by then become very valuable land. They were joined within a few years by the De Repentigny heirs, some of whom were living in poverty in the Caribbean. After several disappointing legal attempts, they obtained passage of a special bill by the U.S. Senate in 1860 authorizing the federal district court in Michigan to decide the validity of their claim. The court ruled in their favor in 1861, but the U.S. Supreme Court reversed the federal court decision in 1867, citing the lapse of time and the failure of the original grantees to improve the land as the primary reason for its decision. Thus ended the last claim to Michigan lands that had once been under French occupation and ownership.

Fort Colyer/Drummond

Drummond Island
1815–1826

Throughout the War of 1812, the British held on to the Straits of Mackinac and their fortress on Mackinac Island. When the Treaty of Ghent was signed on December 24, 1814, ending the war and restoring the original international boundaries, the British were forced to evacuate Fort Mackinac along with the other Upper Midwest posts occupied by the Americans before the war.

The loss of Fort Mackinac was a crushing blow to the interests of the British fur trade. It was the key to their northern operations and necessary for keeping the Natives loyal to the British. It was necessary for the British to select some point on the St. Mary's River system for the location of a military post that would effectively take the place of Mackinac. The British Sault Ste. Marie, on the north side of the St. Mary's River, was low and swampy and considered ill-suited for a military post. St. Joseph Island had advantages but had never been popular with the British, even though they had occupied it at the start of the War of 1812.

The British commander, Lieutenant Colonel Robert McDonall, selected Drummond Island as the best option for a fort location to allow the British to maintain control of the lucrative fur trade, and the fort location would also allow the British to continue their assault on the Native American culture. Using alcohol and other trade goods that the Natives came to depend on, larger and larger bits of Native culture were being lost. Fort Mackinac was still very much on the minds of British commanders; therefore, a fort on Drummond Island was the strategy employed by the British as a toehold, allowing them some influence with the Native population.

Across the DeTour Passage and across from what is now DeTour Village on the mainland is the western shore of Whitney Bay on Drummond Island. Called Pon-tan-ag-an-ipy by the Indians, the island was renamed by the British in honor of Lieutenant General Gordon Drummond. Of the three choices the British considered, it was the closest to Mackinac Island and would allow them to maintain some control of and influence over the fur trade.

The British garrison, of between 350 and 400, set about building a small fort on Drummond Island in 1815 and christened it Fort Colyer, but many referred to it as "Fort Drummond." A number of British soldiers brought their families to the new fort and built homes outside the fort. A separate civilian settlement was also built nearby and called Collyer's Harbor. The Americans would later rename this Whitney Bay.

Several barracks and crude dwellings were quickly erected for immediate shelter, along with storehouses, a hospital, a bakehouse, and other necessary structures. An earthwork shore battery was built on the western end of the island overlooking Portage Bay. By June 1823, there were eighteen buildings constructed by the garrison, not including a number of civilian houses built down by the harbor.

When the British moved to the island and started building the fort, their only real interest was in maintaining the fur trade with the Natives. The British government did not want to give this up, especially to the Americans.

Much of the planned construction of the fort was delayed and ultimately not finished due to McDonall's request not being approved. Therefore, no civilians could be employed, which meant that the soldiers had to do all the work, which was considerable according to the original plan. The construction work continued through the long, cold winter, and many men died from the freezing cold and sickness. The fort was originally supposed to have separate housing for soldiers and civilians. However, due to the slow progress in construction, the separate facilities were never built. The buildings that were constructed were shared by both soldiers and civilians.

Most buildings were made of timber; however, a lime quarry was created, and fireplaces, kitchens, and bakehouses were built using very good quality stone. Some of the remnants of these fireplaces are still standing, which means great care was taken to craft the structures.

By international arbitration in 1822, Drummond Island was declared to officially belong to the United States. The British garrison took its time but finally withdrew in November 1828 and moved to St. Joseph Island on the eastern side of the St. Mary's River.

The British were warned, in advance, that they would have to evacuate, but the early arrival of the Americans found the British unprepared to go on a moment's notice, as they were required to do. The ship assigned to move the garrison was too small to carry the personal possessions of all the troops. There was a great rush to dispose of property that could not be taken, at a great loss to the British. Livestock was virtually given away. The evacuation of Fort Colyer/Drummond in 1826 proved particularly painful for the English soldiers with families. When the fort was originally built, they were compelled to provide their own houses, outside the fort grounds. Most had gardens and shelter for livestock, which they had to leave behind.

Fort Colyer was not immediately filled with an American garrison, but rather was left abandoned. The name Fort Drummond was probably bestowed in the summer of 1827 after the British civilians finally left. Most of the wood structures were still standing as of 1831, but they were then mostly burned down after an 1836 treaty that ceded the land back to a local tribe of Native Americans.

The impact of the American Revolution and the War of 1812 on the Native Americans was huge and long-lasting, due primarily to the way the British commanders drew them into many battles. The British had offered their assistance and resources, but the Natives found them as empty promises. The Native Americans were forced into the war against the Americans with false stories and with false promises. The tribes on Drummond Island were left very much to fend for themselves after the war.

After the British troops left Drummond Island, there was no immediate action taken at the fort by the United States. It remained abandoned for years. Yet despite it being listed in the National Register of Historic Places and designated as a Michigan State Historic Site in 1924, the fort property was divided and sold to private citizens.

It was a number of years after the War of 1812 before white settlers approached the island with any intention of setting up homesteads. The John Seaman family were the first permanent American settlers to arrive on Drummond Island in the early 1850s. They began a farming homestead and a limestone quarry, along with a lumber milling operation. The Seaman family have been credited with settling their homestead and inviting other pioneering families to buy land and set up homesteads for themselves, sometimes with financial assistance from the Seaman family. Today's Seaman family descendants can trace their connection to those very independent pioneers.

Drummond Island was basically one large limestone formation and in some places has a good covering of humus, making it quite productive farmland. Today, at the former site of Fort Colyer/Drummond, the ancient parade grounds can be distinctly traced, for it has only a light covering of moss. Where soil has accumulated, there is a second growth of balsam, birch, and poplar trees. Rows of buildings are evidenced by the fireplaces and chimneys that have survived to this day. They were made from limestone and mortar and have held up well to the harsh weather conditions. One fireplace, larger than the rest, is believed to be the remains of the bakehouse. There are at least three other fireplaces still standing. One has had a home built around it. Two others are still standing by themselves in a small section of hardwood. One other chimney has been relocated to the Drummond Island Historical Museum.

Now, after years of weather abuse, all the land that had been occupied by the old fort is privately owned. The few lasting remnants are preserved from public interference and stand as a reminder of a time when the island and fort were important parts of U.S. history.

The old British graveyard, a few hundred yards from the parade grounds, is virtually untraceable and is now on private property. Some rough stone markers are still there. The cemetery likely holds about three hundred British graves.

The British were not well prepared to make the move from Fort Drummond and were forced to abandon a great deal of personal belongings along with food, furniture, and clothing. Military equipment that could not be loaded on the small boats was left behind. A number of cannons were dumped into the little bay in front of the fort, and for many years visitors to the island searched the clear waters. Cannonballs have been found, and many still lie on the bottom of the bay in small piles.

After the British left, U.S. Army Lieutenant T. Pierce Simonton officially took control of the island and the fort on November 14, 1828. He quickly changed the name of the fort from Colyer to Fort Drummond. Some British civilians stayed on the island hoping to start a new American colony. The U.S. Army abandoned the fort because at the end of the War of 1812, the government in Washington, D.C., decided to disband much of its standing army, as it was not needed if there was no war to fight.

Today, the location of the old Fort Drummond is only visible from the water of Whitney Bay. The fort's historical significance as a British stronghold endures in the lore of Drummond Island. Remains from the fort can be seen at the Drummond Island Museum. The museum's private property holds what is left from the fort after locals opened the property up to tourists, who picked through the remains for anything of value or interest. What is left is now in the museum. The museum also contains Native American artifacts that were used in trading with the British and Native American relics that have been dated from 200 BC.

John Seaman and his wife, Elizabeth, bought the old fort land. They built their home across the road from the fort grounds. The Seaman family built and still operate the Drummond Island Historical Museum.

On the island, there are still many reminders of the old fort, which at one time was intended by the British to be the "Gibraltar of North America."

Fort Croghan/Nonsense

Detroit
1806–1814

In 1806, Fort Croghan was built near what is now the northeast corner of Park and High Street in Detroit. It was circular in form and about forty feet in diameter. It consisted of an earth embankment about ten feet high and two feet wide at the top. There was a solid vertical picket gate made from small cedar saplings that were banded together. It was surrounded by a small ditch and was mounted with a few pieces of artillery.

Early in the nineteenth century, the Indians near the city were continually killing cattle and driving off the horses. To protect the stock, which grazed freely in the area, and to provide a building to protect animal feed storage along with some munitions, Fort Croghan was built next to Fort Shelby and was fortified with a small detachment of infantry. The fort was most often used as training grounds for new recruits who needed small arms or long rifle training. Training new recruits in nighttime military maneuvers, working back and forth between the forts, was thought to be valuable training regardless of the enemy.

When the Native American situation in the Michigan Territory became more stable, Fort Croghan became obsolete. The soldiers of Fort Shelby were ordered to use the now obsolete fort for artillery practice by firing into it from Fort Shelby. The intent was to be able to keep Native Americans out of the fort should they actually try to occupy it.

Fort Croghan/Nonsense was a real fort. It was, temporarily, fortified with soldiers; therefore, it did earn its designation as a bona fide military fort.

In later times, the fort became a favorite place for children to play, choosing up sides and then battling for possession. In all likelihood, it was the children who nicknamed it "Fort Nonsense." Over the course of those childhood battles, many wars were fought, lost, and won, along with life lessons learned. The fort site was later covered over and trampled on and eventually became a forgotten piece of Michigan military history.

Historically, no records exist as to the size, shape, or overall footprint of the military post known as Fort Croghan or Fort Nonsense.

DETROIT (DEARBORN) ARSENAL

Dearborn
1817–1875

In 1817, the Detroit Arsenal was built along the Detroit River within the city limits. The main purpose of the arsenal was to serve as a supply depot for the U.S. Army, storing, maintaining, and repairing arms and munitions. It had been garrisoned by a small detachment of soldiers. The garrison also provided protection from western Native American tribes who were involved in the Black Hawk War. The explosives inventory included small brass cannons, large drums of gunpowder, howitzers, and a tack room filled with horse bridles, saddles, and harnesses.

By 1830, the population of the city had grown quite large, and there was some fear that the stores of explosives could endanger the immediate neighborhoods. The U.S. Congress authorized the construction of a new arsenal at a site on Chicago Road near the River Rouge, west of Detroit in the village that would become Dearbornville.

Construction of the new arsenal began in 1833 and was completed in 1837. From a nearby clay pit, bricks were made and eleven buildings were erected around a square, eight hundred feet on a side. Sawn lumber was sent by barge up the Rouge River, and slate for the roofs was imported from New York. The structures of the Dearborn Arsenal had the first slate roofs in Michigan. Eleven brick buildings were spaced around inside a high brick wall, which made a solid enclosure. It was fortified with a small detachment of regular army and so therefore qualifies as a "fort."

The eleven buildings comprised an armory, sutler's shop, guardhouse, enlisted and officer barracks, surgeon's quarters, carpenter shop, blacksmith shop, saddler tack shop, gun carriage, arsenal headquarters, and commandant's quarters. The powder magazine was built and located outside the walled square, three hundred yards east of the gate.

The arsenal remained active through the American Civil War until 1875, at which time it was closed and sold by the government. The only building that remained in its original location was the commandant's quarters.

In 1899, the armory was converted into a woolen mill; in 1970, the mill was destroyed by fire. The bricks from the old mill were used to build new houses in the neighborhood, some of which still stand today. A record of those houses has been maintained by many local libraries.

The guardhouse, barracks, and surgeon's quarters were used as private residences; in 1893, all three were demolished to build a school. The sutler's shop was remodeled into a doctor office. The carpenter shop and blacksmith shop were combined and turned into a three-unit apartment building. The saddler tack shop was for a while a private residence. Then it was converted into the Dearborn Town Hall. In 1928, the building was sold to S.S. Kresge and was moved to another location. Sadly, it was destroyed by fire in 1946.

The gun carriage building was bought in 1906 by the Masonic Temple and was later used as a dry cleaner business before being used as a bakery. The building used as the powder magazine was bought by Nathaniel Ross and turned into a private residence in 1883; later, it was donated to the City of Dearborn in 1950. It was then moved to its current address at 915 Brady Street and renamed the McFadden-Ross House and used as a museum.

The commandant's quarters, over the years, was used as a library, an American Legion Hall, a town hall, a police station, a school, and a newspaper office. In 1949, the building was purchased by the City of Dearborn and used by the historical commission as a museum. In 1970, it was listed in the National Register of Historic Places. The commandant's quarters is the only building left of the original eleven that is still standing in its original location.

FORT DUBUADE

St. Ignace
1672–1701

In 1671, Father Jacques Marquette arrived at the southern point of the Upper Peninsula at the Straits of Mackinac to live with a band of Hurons. He quickly opened a mission and named it St. Ignace in honor of the Catholic Saint Ignatius. In 1672, French troops led by Louis de la Porte Sieur de Louvigny built a crude fort beside the bay and named it Fort DuBuade, in honor of Count Louis de Buade Frontenac, who had financed the Louvigny expedition into the interior of the continent.

The Natives called the settlement Min-is-ing, meaning "Place of the Big Island," but the mission's name of St. Ignace became its lasting designation.

For nearly forty years, it was the northwestern capital of French trade and Jesuit evangelism.

On May 18, 1675, while returning to his mission at St. Ignace from a trip down the Mississippi River, Father Marquette died and was initially buried on the beach near present-day Ludington, Michigan, on the eastern shore of Lake Michigan. Two years later, his bones were dug up by local Native Americans and transported back to St. Ignace, where his remains were buried beneath the floor of his cherished chapel.

In 1683, in an effort to protect his fur trade interests, the French king requested that a fortification be built that would also enclose the Jesuit mission at St. Ignace. The priests did not want and did not need protection, and the fur trade, at that time, was in no danger from foreign intervention. Soon the troops began trading garrison supplies with the local Natives for beaver pelts, and army deserters became illegal fur traders. Even from the start, fur traders needed to be licensed. Somehow, all the regulations of the king were lost in the wilderness.

The illegal practices by the fur traders caused much tension. In 1683, New France Governor Joseph-Antoine de La Barre ordered Daniel Greysolon, Sieur du Lhut, and Olivier Norel de La Durantaye to take control of the north shore of the Straits of Mackinac. La Durantaye settled in as overall commander of the French forts in the Upper Midwest: Fort Saint Louis des Illinois (Utica, Illinois), Fort Kaministigoya (Thunder Bay, Ontario), and Fort la Tourette (Lake Nipigon, Ontario).

By 1689, the French forts had become a staging area for the French to train local Native tribes to war against the Seneca tribes. The Senecas had aligned themselves with the English, who had started to take advantage of unprotected areas of the French fur trade, when war broke out between the French and the English in 1689. St. Ignace had become an important fur trading center, but the French were having trouble protecting it.

At the end of the war in 1694, the governor of New France sent the young, aggressive Antoine de la Mothe Cadillac to run the post at St. Ignace. The previous commander, La Durantaye, had ruled the Michilimackinac area with a firm hand. He controlled the trade of brandy and furs and tried desperately to keep the traders in line. He was an honest man but would spend the rest of his life in relative poverty.

Cadillac did not hold himself to the standards of La Durantaye. He brought in large supplies of alcohol to be sold and traded at the post, with the profits going into his own pocket. He took many bribes from licensed and unlicensed trading agents. The Jesuit missionaries accused Cadillac of using the brandy to control the Native tribes. That may have been Cadillac's motive, but he explained that it was his strategy to keep the English traders in check. But there is no doubt that this added greatly to his personal finances.

Despite Cadillac's liquor trade, French and English fur trade competition continued. In 1701, Cadillac was replaced as the commander of St. Ignace by Alphonse Tonti. Cadillac had received permission from Paris to establish a new post on the River de Troit to interdict the flow of English trade goods into the Lake Huron area. In the summer of 1701, Cadillac moved a large portion of the garrison from Fort DuBuade south to the Straits of de Troit, leaving a smaller garrison behind with Commander Toni to protect the Straits of Michilimackinac.

The strategic location of the Straits of Mackinac could not be denied. Within a few years, without authority, a new settlement had sprung up, this time at the northern point of the southern peninsula at the Straits, near present-day Mackinac City. Traders, with illegal goods on unlicensed canoes, began gathering there and trading with the Natives.

Between 1701 and 1715, there was no official French presence at the Straits of Mackinac. Unlicensed trading continued during this period until a French army detachment showed up in 1715. Under the command of

Fort DuBuade (1688)
(rendition)

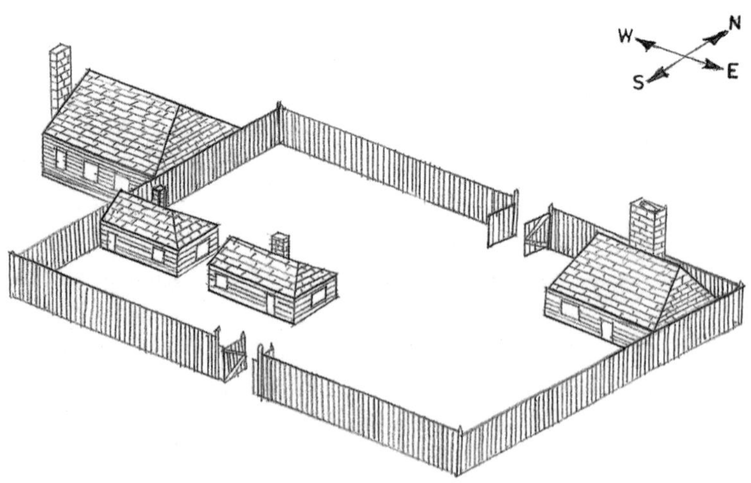

Fort DuBuade (footprint rendering). *Courtesy of author.*

Constant le Marchand de Lignery, the French reestablished control of the Straits of Mackinac. They immediately began work on a new post located on the south shore of the Straits in present-day Mackinaw City. The new post was called Fort Michilimackinac. Once the new fort was built, the old fort and mission at St. Ignace were abandoned and forgotten.

The location of the chapel that guarded the burial site of Father Marquette was lost for many years. In June 1877, a fisherman in St. Ignace was clearing a portion of his land for a garden. Here he discovered the remains of a very old building. Having more than a passing interest in local history, he contacted a historian and soon learned that the building that once stood on his land was the chapel that Father Marquette built in 1671 and also housed his burial site.

When the French built Fort DuBuade in 1672, it was probably constructed as a wooden stockade made of vertical posts embedded in the ground. The exact size and dimensions of the fort are not known, and no physical evidence of the old fort has ever been found. It is believed to have been located at a location within the current city limits of St. Ignace, possibly on a hill above East Moran Bay, locally called Fort Hill. The fort could also have been located on the bay's waterfront. At present, any remains of the fort have not yet been found.

The final fate of Fort DuBuade is unclear. After the new Fort Michilimackinac was completed and the garrison was moved from Fort DuBuade, it is likely that the fort was used to store goods intended for trade with the Natives. Then it was destroyed, burned down, or fell into such disrepair that it could no longer be used.

The Fort Dubuade Museum in downtown St. Ignace is believed to be located on the old fort grounds. The museum houses an extraordinary collection of French and Native American artifacts dating from the early 1600s.

Fort George/Holmes

Mackinac Island
1814–1818

In 1781, British Captain Patrick Sinclair built Fort Mackinac, and it became their chief stronghold in the Northern Great Lakes area. Commanding the area from the bluff overlooking the harbor, the limestone fort was considered impregnable, even though it did not sit on the highest point of the island.

Directly north and behind the fort, rising to a height of 180 feet above the walls of Fort Mackinac, there was a great hill. Although Sinclair recognized the importance of the hill, it was ignored during the construction of Fort Mackinac. The immediate necessity of protecting the harbor and the surrounding village dictated that this could only be accomplished by placing the fort on the bluff between the village and the island's highest point. With the completion of the structure, Captain Sinclair had left the new fort grossly exposed and vulnerable.

In 1788, British Captain Gother Mann arrived at Fort Mackinac and was appalled that seven hundred yards to the north, the great hill totally dominated the fort. By 1788, the British were anticipating the eventual cession of the fort to the United States as was stipulated in the peace treaty, causing further construction to be deemed a waste of labor and money. The great hill that loomed over Fort Mackinac would remain unfortified, but that would soon be corrected.

In September 1796, Mackinac Island was turned over to America. The fatal weakness of Fort Mackinac was not remedied when the Americans took control, even though it was reported to government officials as early as October 1796. It was felt by the government that the harbor and village could only be defended from the existing fort, so the possibility of an enemy attack would have to be risked. The American decision not to fortify the hill proved fateful with the start of the War of 1812.

The British garrison, which had left Mackinac Island and moved to St. Joseph Island, wasted no time in attacking Fort Mackinac. They received word of the new war before the Americans on Mackinac Island and quickly mounted an offensive on July 17, 1812. Landing on the northern shore of the island shortly after midnight, at a spot now called "British Landing," they quietly moved south to the spot on the hill overlooking Fort Mackinac, dragging a single six-pounder cannon. At sunrise, the Americans found themselves looking up at the single cannon barrel sitting on the hill above them. The American commander realized that he had no choice but to surrender. The British had regained the fort and the island without firing a single shot. They immediately set plans into motion to strengthen their position and fortify the commanding hill above the fort.

British Lieutenant Andrew Bulger was tasked with building a fortification on the top of the hill, which was known as "Turtle's Back." Work began in May 1814, and by July, the British commander had reported that the fortification was nearly complete. The only problem left to solve was that of supplying water to the hill. The original plans called for a well to be dug within the walls of the new fort, but this proved to be impossible due to the mountain of rock and limestone that would need to be removed. The commander decided that buckets of waters brought up from the lake would have to suffice.

The new fort was christened Fort George, in honor of King George III.

The British haste in building the new fort was well justified. In July 1814, an American warship sailed into the harbor with the intention of blasting Fort Mackinac off the bluff. After several attempts, they realized that they could not raise their cannons high enough to strike the fort.

The next morning, the American attack force landed on the northern shore of the island, just as the British had done two years earlier, and moved south toward the center of the island. They were met only one mile from the beach by the British. There in the woods and fields of Michael Dousman's farm, the two forces engaged in battle. The Americans were surprised and were forced to retreat. During the battle, U.S. Major Anthony Hunter Holmes was killed, along with a few other soldiers.

The decisive action by British Lieutenant Colonel McDougall repelled the only serious attempt by the United States to regain the island by force.

The British continuously worked to improve the new fort throughout the winter of 1814–15. The extra work, however, proved to be in vain. In March 1815, the British received word that Mackinac Island was to return to the Americans at the conclusion of peace negotiations ending the war. The British officers at Fort Mackinac were appalled that their negotiators in the peace talks could so easily give away this vital piece of property.

On July 18, 1815, U.S. troops formally took control of Mackinac Island and the still incomplete Fort George. Undoubtedly, the name of the fort did not sit well with the Americans. King George III had been their enemy throughout the American Revolution and the War of 1812, which had just ended. The fort was soon rechristened Fort Holmes in honor of Major Anthony Holmes, killed during the unsuccessful American attack on the island.

Relatively little remained to be done to make Fort George defensible. The U.S. garrison completed the fort to the exact plans of the British and, from then on, performed only minor operations of repair work.

The British had skillfully sited Fort George to serve two purposes. Situated on the highest point of the island, it effectively protected the vulnerable rear of Fort Mackinac. Also, while the harbor was not visible from Fort George, its cannons could command the entrance to the bay and the channel between Mackinac Island and the Round Islands. The same guns could sweep the plateau on which Fort Mackinac sat.

Access to Fort George was through a single gateway and was designed to be difficult. The fort was shaped like a horseshoe. The gateway was surrounded by heavy timbers and protected by a ditch. Most of the interior of the fort was occupied by a large two-story blockhouse made from squared timbers. Gunports and musket slits were designed into all the exterior walls of the fort. The fort was outfitted with four twelve-pounder cannons and two spaces for cannons that had shorter range.

U.S. Colonel Anthony Butler stated that Fort Holmes must not be neglected if the government had any intentions of maintaining its possession of Mackinac Island. All realized that the control of the heights by an enemy attack would immediately render the defense of Fort Mackinac futile. After the War of 1812, U.S. plans for the security of Mackinac Island focused on Fort Holmes.

In 1817, engineer Major Charles Gratiot was assigned to Fort Mackinac with the job of designing a new Fort Holmes on its present site. He prepared three designs for a permanent fortification on the hilltop. The designs emphasized the importance attached to Fort Holmes following the War of 1812. The designs received some attention as late as 1843 but were never seriously considered again.

After the War of 1812, the British maintained a garrison on Drummond Island, within fifty miles of Mackinac Island. The British soldiers were considered a serious threat to Mackinac, with the lessons from July 1812 still fresh in their minds. Starting in 1815 and for most of the following three years, Fort Holmes would thus be the most important part of the defense of Mackinac Island.

During its few years of importance, the preservation of Fort Holmes included the completion and maintenance of the original British fort. The U.S. equipped the fort with artillery and a full garrison of troops. However, the troops stationed there were never meant to be permanent.

Despite its importance, Fort Holmes did not have suitable barracks and could serve as little more than a guard post. Captain Benjamin Pierce, brother of future U.S. President Franklin Pierce and commander of the artillery unit at Fort Mackinac, was responsible for the maintenance and protection of Fort Holmes during the years it was active.

From 1815 through 1817, the fort was secured for the winter and then reactivated as soon as warmer weather arrived. The fort was last secured for the winter in December 1817 and was never reactivated. Guns and equipment were gathered and removed in the spring of 1818. The fort was then abandoned and allowed to crumble.

In the mid-1800s, the officers of Fort Mackinac requested and received permission to use the blockhouse of Fort Holmes as a target for artillery practice. Their shots soon tore the blockhouse to pieces.

By the end of the nineteenth century, tourism had become the mainstay of Mackinac Island's economy. In 1895, the island was turned over to the National Park Service and, in the same year, was turned over to the State of Michigan to become its first state park. The upkeep of the large park was a costly affair. Leasing the property and buildings were two ways of producing revenue for repairs and maintenance. The granting of concessions was another.

In the spring of 1898, H.W. Hill was granted a five-year concession for $200 to sell curios at the original site of Fort Holmes. He was followed by other businessmen, and the practice of allowing curios shops at Fort Holmes continued throughout World War I.

The Mackinac Island State Park Commission, which still operates the park, wanted to restore the history of the island and had the Fort Holmes

Fort George/Holmes. *Artist Norman Liljegren.*

blockhouse rebuilt from the remaining original timbers in 1907. For nearly thirty years, the weathered log blockhouse provided a backdrop for early snapshots and tour guide accounts of the War of 1812. In the fall of 1933, the blockhouse was destroyed by fire from an unknown source.

In 1934, the park commission hired two carpenters to build a replica of the blockhouse. This replacement was brief, for within two years it was replaced by the most ambitious re-construction to stand on the site. In 1935, the federal government was asked to help, and through the Works Progress Administration (WPA), a new structure was built on the original site. By the 1960s, signs of dilapidation and decay had become evident, and some minor repairs were made. But the deterioration was far too advanced, and dangerous sections of the fort were dismantled. During the winter of 1968–69, the Fort Holmes blockhouse was once again demolished and reconstructed.

Today, Fort Holmes has regained much of its nineteenth-century charm. Currently, a few tour carriages use the road built by the WPA workers, and only those visitors who have the energy to climb the hill take the time to explore the ruins of the fort that was once considered the most important fortification in the territory.

FORT GRATIOT

Port Huron
1814–1879

On May 11, 1814, during the War of 1812, U.S. Army Major Thomas Forsyth and his detachment from the Second Infantry, along with engineer Captain Charles Gratiot, arrived at the foot of Lake Huron, where they found the remains of the old French post Fort St. Joseph. At the time, the site was occupied by a French Canadian trader/farmer with a small house and about two acres of land under cultivation. This site, at the northern end of the St. Clair River where Lake Huron empties into it, is now occupied by the Blue Water Bridge and the Windjammer Hotel, which was originally the Thomas Edison Inn.

At this location, under the supervision of Captain Gratiot, a new fort was built at a cost of $305.25. It was named Fort Gratiot in honor of its builder.

It had been determined by the U.S. War Department that a fort was needed at this location for a more effective defense of the area. The purpose of the fort was to protect the Upper Great Lakes residents for travel and trade on Lake Huron and the St. Clair River. It was the first fort built by the United States on Michigan soil.

The original fort was constructed entirely of wood logs standing vertically with earth piled up along the base, and the upright timbers formed a stockade approximately 165 feet wide by 495 feet long. It also had a two-story blockhouse as the first building within the walls of the fort.

Charles Gratiot was born on August 29, 1786, in St. Louis, then a small town in what was then the Spanish colony of Louisiana. Gratiot and his cousin Auguste Chouteau were the first two appointees (by President Thomas Jefferson) to the newly established West Point Military Academy.

In 1814, this new fort was the site of a great rendezvous of about six hundred American soldiers and five hundred Ohio militiaman, commanded by Colonel George Croghan, on their way to free Fort Mackinac from the British.

Then, in 1822, with the reductions to the American army, Fort Gratiot was abandoned by the military, and the buildings were turned over to two Presbyterian missionaries by the names of Hart and Hudson, who opened a school for Native Americans and the few remaining whites. The school was closed in 1823, and the site was then totally abandoned. In 1828, troops were again sent to Fort Gratiot, but it had become so dilapidated that it had to be completely rebuilt. The grounds were enlarged and enclosed in a stockade.

In 1832, the deadly Asiatic cholera struck Fort Gratiot. Troops coming from the east, heading for Fort Dearborn in Illinois to help fight the Black Hawk War, were forced to stop at Fort Gratiot. When they arrived in July, two men became ill and died within hours. The troops were then sent by way of water to Fort Dearborn in the Illinois territory. Out of the detachment of 280 men at Fort Gratiot, only 9 remained alive—30 died of cholera and the rest reported missing or deserted. Many townspeople died of cholera also due to the overcrowded conditions at the post hospital. Troops looking for a warm place to sleep wandered through town, passing along the deadly disease. The townspeople closed their homes to the soldiers as they begged for food and help. Many soldiers died and were buried immediately with no attempt to identify them or to contact their families. The actual number of deaths due to the epidemic is believed to be large, but no records have survived.

In 1847, the troops of Fort Gratiot were again withdrawn and sent to fight in the war against Mexico. At the end of the war, a detachment of the Seventeenth Infantry was stationed at Fort Gratiot and remained there until 1879, when the fort was abandoned for the final time.

Early in his U.S. military career, the future Confederate general Robert E. Lee was stationed at Fort Gratiot. Although he did not distinguish himself militarily at the fort, he is remembered for one incident. The unverified story tells us that Lee had a fondness for sweets and did not have much money for indulgence. After having run up a sizable bill at a local bakery, he tried to get out of paying the bill by hiding from the bakery owner. The baker searched the fort and found Lieutenant Lee hiding in a closet in the barracks, whereupon Lee was told to either pay the bill within the hour or the constable would be around to see him. The young officer quickly borrowed money from other officers and wasted no time in settling the delinquent account.

In 1882, the old garrison buildings were torn down, and the land was sold by lots at auction. On May 27, 1882, a skeleton was found beneath the floor of one of the remaining buildings that had been occupied by the post surgeons and their assistants. The skeleton, intact except for the legs, is believed to have been that of an elderly Native American woman. No explanations for the skeleton or subsequent death of the person has ever been offered or requested.

The last flag to fly over Fort Gratiot, bearing thirty-eight stars, is on display at the Museum of Arts and History in Port Huron.

During the time of the last occupation, which ended in 1879, Fort Gratiot had been a mustering point for Michigan troops getting ready to fight in the Civil War. Railroad tracks at the old fort site that carried troops southward to the war were left untouched for many years.

Also during this period, the boyhood home of Thomas Edison was just a short stone's throw from the fort, sitting on a hill overlooking the St. Clair River. Today, the old Edison home site is surrounded by a luxury condominium complex.

Since 1879, the original site of the fort has undergone many changes. After the fort was dismantled, the grounds were leveled off and prepared for the laying of new railroad tracks. The Peerless Cement Company later purchased the property and built a cement plant on the site. The cement plant was closed down in 1976.

Fort Gratiot. *Artist Norman Liljegren.*

The site is now home to the Windjammer Hotel and the Thomas Edison/Grand Trunk Railroad Station, which itself has been designated as a historic building. This is the railroad office out of which young Tom Edison would board the trains to sell his goodies and daily newspaper about the Civil War to travelers.

During its lifetime, Fort Gratiot served as a frontier defense post and as a mustering area for the dispatch of soldiers involved in "domestic trouble spots" throughout the entire northwestern territories.

The grounds on which Fort Gratiot had been built have long ago been churned and turned over by new and subsequent property owners to the point that there is nothing left of the old fort to find. History has relegated its memory to the ages, yet the name "Gratiot," in the local area, has been carried on in numerous ways.

GROSSE ILE STOCKADE

Grosse Ile Island, Wayne County
1815–1817

The island of Grosse Ile was first explored and named by French explorers who were part of the Cadillac exploration team in 1701. This exploration team called it Grosse Ile, meaning "large island" in the French language.

Brothers William and Alexander Macomb, merchants and fur traders from Albany, New York, took ownership of the island, thus becoming the first European American owners of the island. The brothers were of Scotch-Irish ancestry, born in Ireland in the mid-1750s and immigrating with their family to the colony of New York before the start of the American Revolution.

The island's significance grew as the brothers acquired it in 1776, laying the foundations for their financial development. No records exist to show how the Macomb brothers acquired the island—whether they bought it or just took it may never be determined. The fact that they did control the island has never been in legal dispute.

The brothers had the island surveyed in 1819, and it was included into Monguagon Township in 1829. The island remained sparsely populated and an independent community, but it did not gain autonomy until the formation of Grosse Ile Township on October 27, 1914. In the twenty-first century, the island of Grosse Ile is considered an affluent part of the downriver community just south of the city of Detroit.

The stockade fort was built in 1815 by the U.S. Army shortly after the War of 1812 on what would later become the East River Road, just south of Bellevue Road. The fort was garrisoned by detachments of the Fifth Infantry Regiment, quartered in seven log cabins. The job of the regiment was to protect the island's civilian population from any further attacks by British forces from the Canadian side of the Detroit River and also from raids by local bands of Native Americans.

The post stockade was decommissioned by Congress in 1817 and then partly demolished in 1819. Over the next few decades, the remaining structure fell into decay and rotted away. Eventually, it was washed away by the weather and forgotten by time. There are no known drawings or written descriptions of the stockade construct. There is a historical marker on the island to confirm the service and approximate location of the Grosse Ile Stockade.

Today, Grosse Ile, Michigan, is a charming community rich in history and surrounded by the scenic beauty of the Detroit River. Located within Wayne County, this civil township is not just any ordinary place. It's a vibrant island community with roots stretching back to the eighteenth century. Grosse Ile's name was bestowed on it by early French explorers in 1679, encapsulating its essence as the largest island in the Detroit River. Its journey from early settlement to a flourishing township is a tale of transformation, marked by significant events and notable figures that have shaped its identity.

The influence of the Macomb brothers is still visible today, from Macomb Street in the central business district to the historic homes and Westcroft Gardens, underscoring their lasting legacy. The area's rich history is preserved in its landmarks and the vivid tales of its early inhabitants and transformative events that shaped its path.

Comprising several islands, with the main island known simply as "The Island" to residents, this area has evolved from a distant military/trading outpost to a beloved home to more than ten thousand people. The islands blend natural beauty with historical significance, with Grosse Ile's unique geographical setup making it one of Michigan's most treasured locales.

The story of the Grosse Ile Stockade begins long before its official recognition. The Potawatomi tribe, the original inhabitants, called the island Kitcheminishen. The island has seen the flags of France, England, and the United States flutter over the land, each playing a pivotal role in its development. The French were the first Europeans to explore the area, with notable figures such as Father Louis Hennepin contributing to its early history. French soldiers traveling with Cadillac roamed the island hunting and trapping, but it wasn't until the aftermath of the American Revolutionary War that Grosse Ile saw its first actual European settlers, marking the beginning of a new era.

There is a historical marker on the island to confirm the service and approximate location of the Grosse Ile Stockade.

Fort Hogan

St. Joseph County
1832–1832

In 1832, during the early days of the Black Hawk War, word of impending danger reached the white settlement at Nottawa-Sippi Prairie, located in the northern part of St. Joseph County (Michigan), which at that time was the home of the Potawatomi reservation. Fearing that the Potawatomis would join Black Hawk's forces, the white settlers assembled and elected militia leaders and decided to also erect a defensive structure, which they named Fort Hogan after the property owner Daniel Hogan.

There were reports from military couriers that the Potawatomis on the Nottawa Reservation had joined with Black Hawk and that they also were collecting the implements and munitions of war and would soon prove formidable foes in the approaching dangers.

The Potawatomis were able to muster about fifty warriors. They had no guns or ammunition, nor did they have the means to procure them. But the hostile intentions of these Natives were considered a certainty and could not be ignored.

What was to be done in this impending crisis? The number of the guards was increased in the village, the patrols were strengthened, and a meeting of the entire settlement was demanded to deliberate on the public safety, as well as to devise ways of securing it against the inevitable attacks.

A meeting was called for the strong men of the village to be held at the house of Captain Powers, who commanded the militia. The meeting comprised an array of citizen soldiers, armed with rusty cavalry swords, shotguns, rifles, and muskets, all of which, from their appearance, had seen service in former wars, along with former soldiers with soiled and tattered uniforms.

After many speeches and solemn deliberation, it was determined to erect a strong fortification on the lands of Daniel Hogan, located near the east end of Nottawa Prairie, to be known as Fort Hogan.

On the following day, the work began. Plows, scrapers, and ox teams were used, along with hardy manual labor until sunset. Fort Hogan, a vertically palisaded fort, soon rose out of the surrounding earthwork of black prairie soil.

After three weeks, with no real credible threat to the area from Black Hawk, the fort was abandoned. The fort was left for children to play in, acting out the battles they had heard about from their fathers. The honorable Fort Hogan, untested in battle, eventually crumbled and dissolved back into the fertile ground.

The Andrew McMillan family now owns and occupies this farm. The walls of Fort Hogan, which had received the labor of forty strong men in one and a half days, have long since been leveled by the farm plow. The size, shape, and footprint of the fort are unknown. There are no remains of the fort, and there is no site marker to identify the location of where Fort Hogan may have briefly stood.

Fort Lernoult/Shelby/Detroit

Detroit
1778–1827

Fort Lernoult/Shelby/Detroit was of some importance during the War of 1812. The fort bounced back and forth in ownership between the British and Americans, including the surrender of the fort to the British by U.S. General William Hull. While Fort Lernoult did not play a decisive role in the War of 1812, it does stand out in the story of the war as a place where the tug-of-war battle for the Upper Lakes Territory took place and tells the lasting story of how important the territory was to the United States.

Fort Lernoult, built by British Captain Richard B. Lernoult in 1778, replaced the old Fort Pontchartrain, which stood on the Detroit River. During the American Revolution, the British feared that the Americans would move north from the Ohio/Kentucky region and easily capture the old French-built fort. Therefore, they decided to build a new and better fort farther back from the river, where today's Federal Building now stands. As it turned out, the construction of Fort Lernoult was probably not necessary. The American George Rogers Clark, commander of the Kentucky Territory, could not gather enough troops and provisions to mount an attack.

The entrance to the fort was facing the settlement of Detroit, through a passageway underneath some trees, with a drawbridge over a twelve-foot-wide ditch running around the fort. On each side of the entrance was an iron twenty-four-pounder cannon. Each side of the fort was defended by two twenty-four-pounders, and at the corner bastions there were four cannons.

At the time of construction, the fort was situated between the present-day streets of Fort and Lafayette the two blocks between Griswold and Wayne.

The fort was constructed of a four-foot-high pile of tree trunks, topped with eight-foot-long sharpened stakes, all of which were covered with an eleven-foot-high earth embankment, which was twenty-six feet thick at the base. Outside of the embankment was a six-foot-deep ditch that was twelve feet wide. It proved to be as difficult for opposing forces to gain entry as it was for those protecting the fort to exit.

Although the British had promised to abandon their forts that were in U.S. territory following the end of the Revolutionary War in 1783, they did in fact continue to occupy six fortifications, two of which were in the Michigan Territory: Fort Lernoult and Fort Mackinac. President Washington sent Chief Justice John Jay to London in 1794 to negotiate a resolution.

In 1795, Jay, on behalf of the United States, signed a treaty with England that would later be called the "Jay Treaty." One of the provisions of the treaty was that all Northwest posts still held by the English were to be given up to the Americans by June 1, 1796.

On July 10, 1796, U.S. troops in two ships landed and camped on the banks of the Raisin River and raised the first American flag on Michigan soil. The next day, three hundred troops arrived at Fort Lernoult under the command of Colonel Jean-François (or John Francis) Hamtramck. At noon, the Union Jack was lowered and the Stars and Stripes was raised. Thirteen years after the signing of the Treaty of Paris, ending the American Revolution, the United States took formal possession of the Michigan Territory. This was to be the closing act of the American war for independence.

Fort Lernoult was renamed Fort Detroit by Secretary of War Henry Dearborn in 1805.

The first American commander at Fort Lernoult/Shelby/Detroit was Colonel Hamtramck. Under his command was a garrison of three hundred soldiers.

In 1807, Michigan Territorial Governor William Hull expanded the fort and raised the stockade walls to a height of fourteen feet, later adding a six-foot-deep, twelve-foot-wide ditch around the entire fortification.

When the War of 1812 was declared, Hull was named a brigadier general and placed in command of the Army of the Northwest. In July 1812, Hull and his forces left Fort Lernoult to conduct an invasion of Canada, which he abandoned once he learned that the British had captured Fort Mackinac.

British commander General Isaac Brock set up artillery batteries in what is now Windsor, Ontario, directly opposite Fort Detroit. Brock had under his command 1,300 soldiers, 2 warships, and 600 Native warriors. On August 15, 1812, Brock sent a demand to Hull with an implicit threat of a massacre. The message from Brock read, "Sir, the force at my disposal authorizes me to require of you the immediate surrender of Fort Detroit. It is far from my inclination to join in a war of extermination, but the Natives will be beyond my control the moment the contest commences."

Initially, Hull refused to surrender, replying, "Sir, I have received you letter and I have no reply to make other than to inform you that I am prepared to meet any force which may be at your disposal and any consequence which may result from the exertion."

The following morning, under the covering fire of their cannon batteries and the warships, the British crossed the Detroit River and began advancing on the fort. American casualties began to mount, and fearing a slaughter at the hands of the Native Americans, Hull surrendered the fort and all weapons.

It is important to illustrate all the damage that the surrender of Fort Detroit caused to the United States, the fort soldiers, and the families living at the fort. Many soldiers died gruesomely during the surrender in front of their wives and children. The British took many of the soldiers as prisoners of war and sent them and their families to Canada on British ships—some of the children were as young as five years old.

General Hull was later court-martialed for surrendering the fort without a fight, accused of a cowardly surrender, found guilty, and sentenced to be shot. He was later pardoned by President James Madison. While his sentence had been remitted, Hull remains, to this day, the only U.S. general to ever have been sentenced to death by an American court-martial.

FORT LERNOULT/SHELBY/DETROIT REMAINED UNDER British control for more than a year, until the British naval defeat on Lake Erie, which effectively ended the War of 1812. The British had also received word that General William Henry Harrison was advancing on Detroit with more than one thousand troops especially trained in advanced warfare. The Americans took control of the fort on September 29, 1813, and the fort was again renamed as Fort Shelby in honor of Kentucky Governor Isaac Shelby, who had come to the aid of General Harrison with a regiment of well-trained volunteers.

When the war ended in 1814, nearly 1,300 soldiers were stationed at the fort. The Treaty of Ghent, signed by the United States and England ending the war, stated that the boundaries between the United States and Canada would not be fortified. But it was not until May 27, 1826, eleven years later, that the two remaining companies of U.S. troops at the fort were reassigned to Green Bay, leaving Detroit, for the first time, without military troops.

War always leaves a heritage of bitterness for its combatants. Sensing this, some leading citizens of Detroit, after the peace had been restored, were determined to erase memories of the recent war as quickly as possible. On May 29, 1815, they gave a "Pacification Dinner" at which former British foes from across the river sat down peacefully with Detroiters. The resumption of friendly relations between British and American neighbors was made easier by this gracious gesture.

In 1892, railroad car manufacturer Charles Lang Freer built a new house at 33 Ferry Avenue in Detroit near today's Wayne State University campus. By this time, Freer had amassed one of the finest art collections in the city, which included a substantial number of etchings, drawings, and lithographs. One piece of art Freer was particularly proud of was a watercolor by the famous American artist James Abbott McNeill Whistler.

The Whistler family enjoyed a strong family connection to Detroit and the fort. The artist's grandfather Major John Whistler was stationed with the U.S. Army at Fort Lernoult from 1797 to 1803. Major Whistler was loved by his men, but they teased him as well, calling him "Red Coat Johnny" because of his service with the British army during the American Revolution. He became an American citizen in 1784.

When he arrived in Detroit in 1797, the responsibility for the safety and security of Fort Lernoult, with only a small military force, was huge. Major Whistler shared his concerns for the fort with the fort commander Colonel John Hamtramck. They both knew that whoever controlled the Straits of Detroit that connected Lakes Erie, Lake St. Clair, and Lake Huron had the upper hand to control the Upper Midwest. Fort Lernoult needed to be ready to repel any invasion by the British should they renege once more in their treaty obligation.

Married to the daughter of an English baron, Major Whistler took his large family to his Fort Lernoult posting. While only one of his children was born in Detroit, the rest of Major Whistler's family, including George Washington Whistler, father of the future artist, fell in love with Detroit. All the children spoke three languages, so growing up in a mostly French-speaking town posed no problems for them.

In 1811, Major Whistler returned from a temporary assignment to Chicago. His return proved to be timely, as the British were hungry to reclaim some U.S. territory and the War of 1812 was about to erupt. Starting in 1812, three successive battles took place just south of Detroit in Brownstown; Maguaga, which was a Wyandotte village; and Frenchtown, now known as Monroe. Two of Major Whistler's sons, already commissioned in the U.S. Army, fought in the Battle of Maguaga. Lieutenant William Whistler survived. John Whistler, a recent West Point graduate, did not. He died on the battlefield.

At Fort Lernoult, the new Michigan territorial governor and military commander General William Hull assessed the results of the battles of Maguaga and Brownstown and deliberated on his ability to protect the town's civilian population. He doubted that his small garrison could be defended against the powerful British force. In a fateful decision that Whistler and other army personnel thought was shameful, General Hull surrendered Fort Lernoult in the face of a British siege.

In 1814, Major Whistler retired from the army and took a series of jobs in Kentucky and Missouri until his death in 1829. Two of Major Whistler's daughters remained in Detroit, and each married successful businessmen. Sarah Whistler married James Abbott Jr., a wealthy fur trader, city trustee, postmaster, and chief judge. He was also a slave owner, owning a man named Pompey, who was enslaved his entire life until his death in 1814.

In 1805, seven years before the War of 1812, a raging fire completely burned all of Detroit to the ground. Sarah and James survived the fire and prospered. Sarah was at the top of the social circle in Detroit. After the War of 1812, Detroit was not considered a wild town on the edge of the frontier. There was a great deal of sophistication to living in Detroit.

Even with that, the artist James Abbott McNeill Whistler was in no hurry to leave London. Charles Freer made numerous trips to London to persuade Whistler to return to Detroit, where Whistler had grown up and where he had created many fine pieces of artwork representing Detroit. Ultimately, the famous artist never did return to the city of his youth.

The grounds of old Fort Lernoult were given to the City of Detroit by Congress, and the old barracks and other buildings were sold and moved away. In the spring of 1827, the stockade was removed and the fort was demolished. The ditch surrounding the fort was filled in at a cost of $625, and the six thousand pickets from the fort were sold at $2 per hundred.

In the spring of 1873, John Owen on Fort Street West was excavating a clearing for his home and found the stump of the flagstaff from Fort Shelby that had been blown down by a storm on April 19, 1818. The staff snapped off at the ground level and was covered over. The stump is now on display

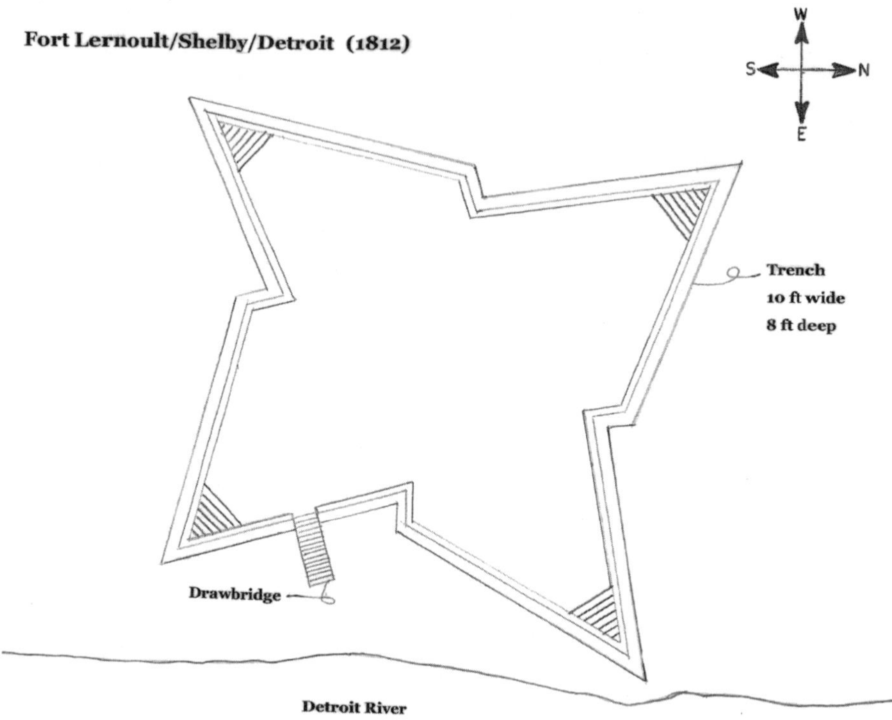

Fort Lernoult/Shelby/Detroit (footprint rendering). *Courtesy of author.*

at the Detroit Public Library. It is the only known structural remnant of Fort Lernoult/Shelby. Before the old fort site was developed, more than eight thousand artifacts were retrieved and are now housed at the Anthropology Museum at Wayne State University.

The fort site was situated at today's intersection of Fort Street and Shelby Street. Today, that corner is occupied by the Theodore Levin U.S. Courthouse, the western portion of the Penobscot Building, the former Federal Reserve Bank of Chicago Detroit Branch Building, and other commercial buildings.

FORT MACKINAC

Mackinac Island
1779–1873

In the fall of 1779, during the American Revolution, British Captain Patrick Sinclair arrived at Fort Michilimackinac and found it to be in almost total disrepair. He quickly assessed the fort's condition and strategic location and determined that the fort and garrison were dangerously exposed and that the fort was virtually defenseless against attack.

Because the fort and trading post had been there for many years, all the surrounding timber had been used. Wood for heating and construction had to be procured from distant locations and islands.

Sinclair, well aware of the American rebellion going on in the East and fearing an attack from George Rogers Clark from Kentucky, decided that the best way to protect the British trading interests in the Great Lakes region was to build a new fort. The day after his arrival at Fort Michilimackinac, he sailed to nearby Mackinac Island, accompanied by a mason, a carpenter, and a farmer. They toured the island, enjoying the view from the plateau 150 feet above the lake.

They tramped through the woods, inspected the natural harbor, and noted the abundance of limestone, which was ideal for building the kind of fortification Sinclair had in mind. Four days later, Sinclair sent a request to Montreal asking for permission to build a new fort on the island and relocate the garrison.

Captain Sinclair knew that it would be many months before he would receive a reply from Montreal, so he ordered construction on the island fort to begin immediately. The first building on Mackinac Island was a transplanted structure from Fort Michilimackinac and used as sleeping quarters and for storage as new structures were built.

Fort Mackinac has the unique history of being the only military fort built on Michigan soil composed chiefly of limestone. The fort was designed to withstand cannon fire. Its thick walls were constructed from limestone quarried from island bedrock formations bonded with lime mortar created in limekilns. Prior to Fort Mackinac, every fort was built out of rough sawn timbers or logs. The fort was completed in 1780, and the British garrison then abandoned Fort Michilimackinac after burning the few buildings that had not been moved and were still standing.

Fort Mackinac was by design separated from the civilian community by sitting on the bluff 150 above the harbor, but the cannon placements selected by Captain Sinclair were located so they could fire down into the main streets and the palisade of the town if necessary during an attack or invasion. Even with that careful planning, Captain Sinclair failed to adequately judge the fort exposure to the large hill that overlooked the back side of the new fort.

The British realized that the new fort on the island commanded the Straits of Mackinac far beyond their initial assumptions. But as it turned out, the construction of Fort Mackinac was actually unnecessary to British interests, as U.S. Colonel George Rogers Clark could not obtain adequate supplies or troops with which to mount an attack on Michilimackinac.

In 1796, the Jay Treaty was signed, ending British occupation of the western posts. One of the last areas to be forfeited by the British was Fort Mackinac in October 1796. They understood the great importance and strategic location of the fort sitting on top of Mackinac Island. The British withdrew their troops from Mackinac Island and moved to St. Joseph Island to the northeast of Mackinac. The American flag was then raised over Fort Mackinac.

When a declaration of war against England was proclaimed by President Madison, beginning the War of 1812, the English used the troops on St. Joseph Island to launch their attack on Fort Mackinac.

When Mackinac Island was first being inspected by Sinclair as a site for a fort, he disregarded the large hill overlooking the site he selected for the new fort. This oversight by the British would prove to be a blessing for them and disastrous for the Americans.

The English commander gathered a force of one thousand troops and Indians from St. Joseph Island and prepared them for the attack on Fort Mackinac. Early on the morning of July 17, 1812, the British force landed on the north side of Mackinac Island, at a spot now called "British Landing," and moved south across the island to a large hill overlooking the back of Fort Mackinac. At daybreak, the British were ready to attack, but no attack was necessary. U.S. Lieutenant Porter Hanks, commander at Fort Mackinac, unaware of the declaration of war, was caught completely off guard. Lieutenant Hanks, realizing that he was badly outnumbered by at least ten to one and while looking up into the throat of a cannon, was forced to surrender. Fort Mackinac passed back into the hands of the English.

When the United States first took control of the fort in 1796 at the end of the American Revolution, the incoming U.S. commander realized the significance of the hill overlooking the fort. He sent messages to his superiors for permission to fortify the hill. Permission was denied. Military leaders, at the time, thought that it would be a waste of time and money. The British, knowing full well the importance of that hill, used it to their advantage to regain control of the fort at the beginning of the War of 1812.

Two years after the British regained control of Fort Mackinac, an American naval force sailed into the harbor, preparing to blast Fort Mackinac off the bluff. However, they soon discovered that their ship's guns could not be raised up high enough to hit the fort. The soldiers on the ship, commanded by Lieutenant Croghan, disembarked on the north side of the island, the same spot the British used to launch their successful attack two years earlier. But the British troops were ready for this and repelled the invaders after a hard battle. After the smoke cleared, the Americans counted sixty-four casualties, including a promising young officer, Major Andrew Holmes. Shortly after this battle, the British built Fort George on the hill behind Fort Mackinac to protect against any American attacks from the north.

British troops held on to the island through the War of 1812 but soon learned that they had lost the war and the island. The Treaty of Ghent was signed on December 24, 1814, ending the war and restoring the original international boundaries that existed before the war. Mackinac Island would again become U.S. property. On July 18, 1815, the British withdrew from Fort Mackinac and moved to Drummond Island, where they built Fort Colyer. A boundary survey in 1822 proved that Drummond Island was also U.S. property, so the British had to move again. This time they moved to St. Joseph Island. When the United States retook control of Mackinac Island after the War of 1812, they renamed Fort George in honor of Major Holmes.

After the War of 1812, the Americans set about constructing three stone blockhouses at Fort Mackinac to serve as living quarters for the enlisted soldiers and to protect against cannon and musket fire.

American John Jacob Astor had started the American Fur Company on Mackinac Island in 1809 to compete with the British traders. This was the beginning of the fabulous Astor fortune. The War of 1812 halted trade for a while, but it resumed shortly after the end of the war. Astor was able to gain the support of the U.S. Congress, and a law was passed stating that only U.S. citizens would be licensed to trade with the Native trappers.

Astor brought hundreds of clerks to Mackinac Island from all over the country. Here, they cleaned, sorted, and counted pelts. By 1820, seven out of every eight traders worked for American Fur Trading Company. Astor had a good business sense and took full advantage of this unbelievable

Fort Mackinac (1779)

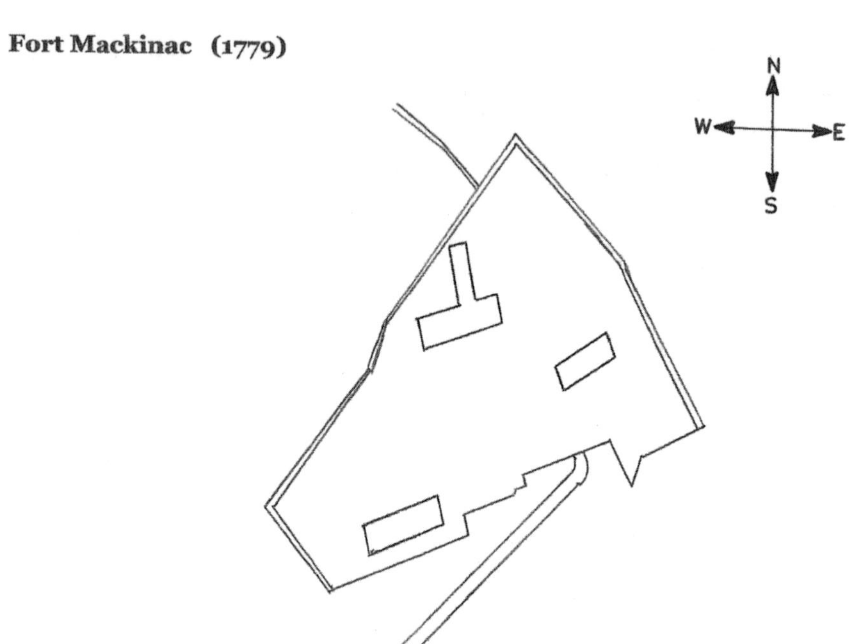

Fort Mackinac (actual footprint). *Courtesy of author.*

opportunity. When he felt that the beaver supply was running out, he sold the trading company and left the area, taking with him the huge fortune he had made.

In 1835, a two-family framed officers' quarters was built directly on the north wall line of the fort. Its placement outside the defensive walls confirmed that Fort Mackinac was no longer at risk of attack. During the next thirty years, many buildings were constructed, along with a two-story barracks and a two-story hospital. In 1867, a quartermaster's storehouse was constructed on limestone foundations and was connected to the post headquarters by a short passageway.

The limestone powder magazine, built in 1780, was demolished, and its walls were then incorporated into the basement of the commissary building. In 1879, a post schoolhouse was built and attached to an outside fort wall. In 1885, with a growing concern for military sanitation and hygiene, a post bathhouse was built.

By 1850, Fort Mackinac was little more than a tourist attraction. It would get a brief assignment for training soldiers during the Civil War, but beyond that, Fort Mackinac had no military importance. The fort that had once commanded the Straits of Mackinac, was the center of the fur trading industry, and witnessed the arrival of hundreds of canoes each year filled with valuable cargo now watched the arrival of boats filled with tourists.

Fort Mackinac is symbolic of the men who built it and a testament to the hard work and dedication to all those who served and died there. The fort changed hands several times since it was built, and it serves as a reminder to the vision and engineering capabilities of British Captain Patrick Sinclair. An interesting note here is that prior to his arrival at Michilimackinac, Captain Sinclair had built a small fort at the mouth of the Pine River where it empties into the St. Clair River, where he owned a one-thousand-acre property that he lovingly referred to as "the Pinery."

On March 11, 1873, U.S. Senator Thomas W. Ferry, who had grown up on the island, proposed a bill to make Mackinac Island a national park. Congress passed the bill in 1875 and transferred the island ownership to the State of Michigan, to be preserved as a state park. In 1894, the last of the federal troops left the island.

Fort Miami

St. Joseph
1679–1779

In 1672, one historical account credits Father Allouez with discovering the St. Joseph River where it empties into Lake Michigan. A large cross has been placed there in his memory. Other accounts give the credit for the discovery of the river to Father Jacques Marquette in April 1675.

One fact that is not disputed is that the famous French explorer René-Robert Cavelier, Sieur de La Salle, was present in 1679. During that year, La Salle and his crew constructed Fort Miami at the mouth of the river. The settlement that grew up around the fort was called Saranac and then Newburyport and then finally St. Joseph.

When La Salle hoisted the French flag and claimed for France all the land he traveled through, he marked the formal opening of the vast area to the south and west as being the sovereignty of the French king.

La Salle had initially landed at the St. Joseph River in his ship the *Griffin*, which was the first sailing vessel on the Upper Lakes. Here, at the mouth of the St. Joseph River, he and part of his crew traded with the local Native Americans. After traveling along the southern coastline of Lake Michigan, La Salle accumulated a large cargo of furs in trade with the local Natives. It was then decided by La Salle that half of his crew would sail the *Griffin* back to Lake Erie and then transport the cargo overland to Montreal. After this was completed, the crew would then sail the ship back to the mouth of the St. Joseph River to pick up La Salle and the rest of the crew.

While waiting for the return of the *Griffin* from its run to Montreal with the load of beaver pelts, La Salle and his men built a fort and christened it Fort Miami. The *Griffin* did not return by a time that La Salle had determined should have been sufficient. When La Salle realized that the *Griffin* would not be returning, he and his remaining crew burned Fort Miami to the ground and set out on foot for Montreal, across and through the lower Michigan forest and swamp.

At this point in history, the fate of the *Griffin* can only be guessed. Most historians believe that the ship went down in a storm on northern Lake Michigan west of the Straits of Mackinac. La Salle believed that the crew stole the valuable cargo and then scuttled the ship to cover the theft. Although there have been numerous efforts of underwater salvage companies with historical interests plying the waters every summer and fall, to date no evidence of the *Griffin* has been found.

The French returned to the mouth of the St. Joseph River and rebuilt the fort in 1681. Then in 1700, the fort was enlarged by a visiting Jesuit missionary, and it remained in French possession until the French and Indian War, at which point it was conquered by the British.

Fort Miami then came under the command of British Colonel John Colonel, who with a handful of soldiers resisted regular attacks by surrounding Native American tribes. The fort fell to the local tribes during Pontiac's Rebellion in May 1763. However, before the end of the year, the fort would return to British control.

Fort Miami would become a centralized fur trading center operated by a Frenchman named Jean Baptiste Marcot, a trader and chief agent for the Northwest Fur Company. He was later murdered in 1783 by a drunk Native American with whom Marcot had bartered alcohol for furs. Marcot's wife, Marguerite Magdelaine Marcot, took over the trading center and expanded the business when possible, becoming a very wealthy widow as a result of her expertise.

Fort Miami is remembered as the first military fortification built on Michigan soil strictly for defensive reasons rather than as a mission or a trading post. The only evidence left for Fort Miami is a historical marker planted near the river in the city of St. Joseph.

Fort Michilimackinac

Mackinaw City
1715–1781

Six years after the French abandoned Fort DuBuade, in 1700, they again realized the strategic importance of the Straits of Mackinac. A trading settlement on the southern tip of the Straits, near present-day Mackinaw City, began to grow. It was made up mostly of French traders and local Natives.

In 1701, Cadillac pulled the garrison out of Fort DuBuade and moved south to the Detroit River, abandoning the fort at St. Ignace. French fur traders with illegal goods on unlicensed canoes continued to do business with the Natives, on a limited basis at first, despite the French abandonment of the area.

The importance of the Straits, which were the crossroads for traders and trappers traveling to and from the North and West, could not be overlooked. Due to this, in about 1715, the French built Fort Michilimackinac. The main palisade outer walls were made up of twelve-foot vertical cedar logs with small bastions at each corner of the mostly square construction. The small company of troops also built structures inside the walls of the fort, which included a headquarters building plus barracks for both officers and enlisted personnel. French traders built a trading post and personal huts outside the gates of the fort.

By 1722, there were thirty French families of soldiers and officers inside and thirty families of French traders outside the gate. The soldiers served three-year terms, and many signed on again because life in the area, for the most part, was pleasant. The soldiers received no pay and had to buy their own uniforms, but they were issued powder and bullets and were free to trade these with the Indians. Many soldiers, upon departing the fort, took packs of furs with them to Montreal. By 1750, one soldier had served thirty years at Fort Michilimackinac and another soldier twenty years.

In the spring of 1749, the French commissioned military engineer Michel Chartier de Lotbiniere to chart an accurate route to Michilimackinac using the most modern survey skills available. The governor of New France had come to realize that he could not rely on the numerous reports of the route made by others, which contained enormous contradictions.

The formal report by de Lotbiniere has been lost to time; even though a draft of the manuscript exists, the last four pages have not survived. A translated version, containing many of de Lotbiniere's corrections and additions, is all that has survived. When he arrived at Fort Michilimackinac, he set to work making a drawing of the fort footprint. He went on to describe in detail the construction issues that made the fort vulnerable. He felt that the walls were too short and that the bastions were too small. He also had concerns that the fort was built on sand that was much too close to the water. He felt that erosion would lead to its downfall. De Lotbiniere also noted that the powder magazine inside the fort was buried and covered with turf. He noted that the forty poorly constructed houses inside the fort were built using horizontal logs and caulked inside and out with clay. The church inside the fort was built with milled timbers, which required little caulking.

De Lotbiniere's report paid little or no attention to the Native Americans with whom his country was involved in active trade. He gave no descriptions of the people or the living conditions as he saw them. His final report described the fort conditions and the surrounding land. On October 7, de Lotbiniere began his trip back to Montreal.

The Jesuit priests of Michilimackinac owned their own property and had a steady income through their control of the blacksmith business, charging the Natives and Frenchmen alike for repairs on guns and traps and the forging of spears and anchors.

The woodworkers, blacksmiths, and other artisans at the fort created a wide variety of articles for daily household use and for trade. Historical records show that boat building was one of the most common jobs to be found; even though no remains of actual boats have been found by archaeologists, the sales of many boats had been recorded in inventories. The blacksmiths were kept especially busy with patrons wanting a wide variety of metal materials from fishhooks to spears and items used in daily life. Sheet brass was an extremely versatile material that lends itself well to the smithing process. Many items have been uncovered in the sands of Fort Michilimackinac showing just how well the artisans worked.

The battle between England and France for control of the New World's wilderness ended when Quebec and Montreal were taken by the English in 1759. England took possession of New France after 150 years of French domination.

The English officers treated the Natives with open contempt, and the English traders swindled them at every opportunity. The first English garrison at Fort Michilimackinac lasted little more than four years. On a day in early June 1763, more than half of the garrison was massacred by the Natives in the "Conspiracy of Pontiac." Caught completely off guard by the attack, the soldiers could do little to defend themselves.

At the time of the attack, the fort was under the command of Captain Etherington and was guarded by ninety-three soldiers. Although Etherington had been warned of the danger of a Native attack, he paid little attention to it even as groups of Natives started gathering around the fort. He felt that they were behaving in a friendly manner and represented no danger.

The soldiers were invited by the Native players to watch a lacrosse match, and as it was the king's birthday, they were in a holiday spirit. Carelessly, the soldiers wandered out of the fort palisade to watch the game as it progressed. The game continued for some time. As it did, Native women had lined up against the fort wall just outside of the gate with weapons hidden under their clothing and blankets, completely unnoticed by the soldiers.

At about noon, a Native player pitched the ball high into the air and over the walls and into the fort. This was the signal for the Natives to attack. As if still playing the game, they dashed through the open gate after the ball. Once inside, the players grabbed up the weapons the Native women had hidden under their clothing and under blankets, and the massacre began. Before the soldiers had time to react, more than half of them were killed, and by then it was too late to do anything. Captain Etherington and the remaining soldiers were taken prisoner, and after weeks of torture and suffering, they were released.

After the attack, the Natives wandered throughout the fort, taking what they wanted and then burning a portion of the fort to the ground. A full year passed before the English were able to secure the area of Michilimackinac and build another fort.

In 1766, Major Robert Rogers, the newly appointed governor commandant of Michilimackinac, arrived with bold ambitions. Major Rogers was the leader of "Rogers Rangers," a group of men who dressed like frontiersmen, carried rifles like white men and tomahawks like Natives, and believed that they could go anywhere that a Native could go and whip anyone they found there. The arrogance of this group was widely known.

Major Rogers understood the mentality of the Native Americans and the surrounding wilderness as no other Englishman did. The British authorities could have saved themselves a great deal of trouble if they had left the matters of the Great Lakes region in his hands. But the authorities did not realize just how well Rogers knew and understood the Natives, which proved very costly indeed.

Rogers had orders to confine trade to the fort itself so that the Natives would not be cheated. Having always been impatient, he took immediate steps to set up a system by which the entire fur country, which was everything beyond Detroit's immediate reach, would be under the control of the government back in England, with whom the governor of Michilimackinac would deal directly. The governor of Michilimackinac, of course, was Major Rogers himself.

Rogers promised the Natives that he would protect them from illegal white traders and that trade goods they wanted would be delivered to them by his men working out of Michilimackinac. The Natives liked this idea, but Rogers's superiors did not. They believed that he was trying to set up his own empire in order to strike a deal with France or Spain. Rogers was widely known as an ambitious man with many grand notions, but he could not convince his superiors that he had only the interests of England at heart.

Rumors of his dealings began to spread, and before long, the officials in Montreal heard of his extravagances, personal ambitions, and disregard of orders. He ran up huge debts in his name as well as in the name of the British Crown.

In 1768, Rogers was recalled to Montreal, accused of high crimes, and brought to trial. He was eventually acquitted of all charges, but the damage to his reputation was permanent. His career was over. He returned to England and died a broken man.

John Askin, of Scotch-Irish descent, had been working as the fort commissary and as a fur trader since 1764. In December 1778, he decided that he needed to make a written inventory of his assets and liabilities. Askin was a highly intelligent man who recognized the value of keeping accurate records. The timing of Askin's records has become significant in that the fort would shortly become abandoned and covered by the sand.

Askin operated a large farm three miles from the fort. To maintain the farm, he owned and worked six slaves, two of whom were black. Their names are listed as Pompey and Jupiter. He also had four Native American slaves for whom he had traded, three of whom were girls between the ages of nine and seventeen. The Askin farm inventory also included a number of milk cows, oxen, horses, pigs, and chickens. The farm equipment consisted of a scythe, hoes, shovels, rakes, hay forks, two wheelbarrows, and a machine to cut oats. Askin also employed a blacksmith to create and repair the farm tools. He was a businessman and devoted eight pages of his fort trading post inventory to his stocks of merchandise, with the majority earmarked for trade with the Natives. A major part of his trade inventory, not surprisingly given his roots, was a generous quantity of whiskey and rum. When the military moved from Fort Michilimackinac to the new Fort Mackinac, trader John Askin moved with them.

Due to the beginning of the American Revolution back east, the Great Lakes region received few supplies, and communication was all but cut off. The fort fell into disrepair. Sand hills piled up behind the fort, blown there by the relentless wind. Sandbars blocked the small bay, and ice mangled the boat landings.

In the fall of 1779, Captain Patrick Sinclair arrived at this rickety post, somewhat unwillingly, but with ambitions of his own. If the ambitions of Major Rogers were personal, those of Captain Sinclair were almost entirely for the British Crown.

Immediately after careful inspection of the fort, Captain Sinclair pointed his telescope at the white-walled limestone formation known as Mackinac Island. Due to the American Revolution and the threat of attack by the American George Rogers Clark, commandant of the Kentucky Territory, Captain Sinclair decided to build a new fort. Four days after he arrived at Fort Michilimackinac, he sent a message to Montreal asking for permission to build a new fort on Mackinac Island and to move the garrison.

Detailing his plans for a new post and pointing out the strategic advantages of the island, he went to work on the new fort immediately, with total confidence that his request would be granted. He traveled to the island, mapped the terrain, and began construction on the bluff overlooking the natural harbor of the island.

In 1781, the new fort was completed, and the garrison was moved to the island. Old Fort Michilimackinac was abandoned. As it turned out, the new fort was unnecessary, at least as far as Sinclair's fear of an American attack was concerned, but later it proved to be invaluable to the British during the War of 1812.

Within a few years, the crumbling Fort Michilimackinac was covered by the shifting sands of the Straits of Mackinac and was left untouched until a twentieth-century archaeological expedition uncovered and restored it. Even with the strategic importance of the location of Fort Mackinac on

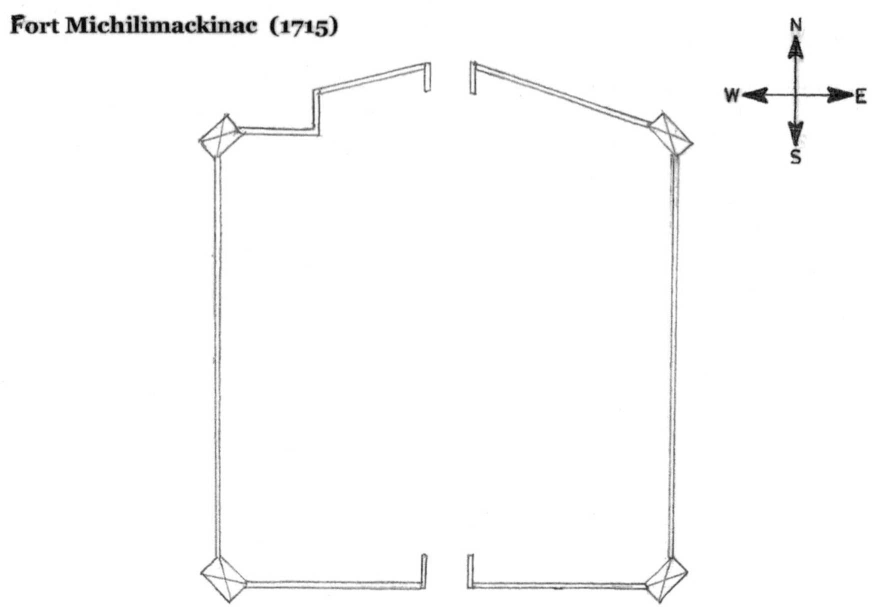

Fort Michilimackinac (actual footprint). *Courtesy of author.*

the island bluff, thousands of tourists each year are drawn to the rebuilt Fort Michilimackinac, where a continuous archaeological effort is watched closely by visitors.

FORT PONTCHARTRAIN DETROIT

Detroit
1701–1778

In 1701, the French conceived the idea of building a fort at what would later become Detroit. The French military commanders had determined that there was no other way they could protect and control their fur trade in the northwest. Only through the control of this area could they prevent the English from trading with the Natives. The French also wanted to protect the tribes of friendly Natives from the constantly warring Iroquois.

In early June 1701, Cadillac and about one hundred settlers and soldiers set out from Fort DuBuade. The expedition reached Grosse Isle in the Detroit River near the end of July. The expedition then turned back upriver several miles to a bluff on the west shore of the river at its narrowest point. Cadillac then began the construction of a fort that he named Fort Pontchartrain du Detroit in honor of Count Pontchartrain, who had helped Cadillac get funding for the expedition from King Louis XIV. They also built a chapel in honor of Saint Anne, the patron saint of New France. In September, Cadillac's wife and the wife of his lieutenant arrived as the first two European women in Detroit.

The original small structure was built from white oak, twelve feet in height, and the total enclosure was less than an acre. A settlement based on the fur trade, farming, and missionary work slowly developed in the area. Fort Pontchartrain was located in what is now downtown Detroit, just northeast of the intersection of Washington Boulevard and West Jefferson Avenue.

The area enclosed by the fort included all the land between present-day Woodbridge Street on the south to about Larned Street on the north and from Griswold Street on the east to Wayne Street on the west.

This site was chosen to enable the French to control all traffic on the Detroit River and hopefully control travel to the Upper Lakes region. After the fort site was chosen, Natives from the Ottawa and Wyandot tribes migrated to Detroit and helped build palisaded villages around the fort. In 1705, Cadillac reported in his journal a Native population of nearly two thousand.

The population of the fort, during construction, consisted of fifty soldiers, fifty artisans (blacksmiths/gunsmiths), and two priests. The fort was built on the banks of the Detroit River, next to a stream called the Savoyard, which is now part of an underground sewage system.

In 1707, Cadillac began granting land in the vicinity of the fort to French settlers. He required that they pay greatly inflated annual rents and a percentage of their crops to him. In response to the complaints about Cadillac's financial practices, Count Pontchartrain appointed François Clairambault d'Aigremont to investigate the conditions at Detroit. In November 1708, d'Aigremont accused Cadillac of profiteering and establishing policies that threatened the French control of the Upper Midwest. The report described Cadillac's rule as that of a tyrant and added that Cadillac had earned the hatred of the French settlers and their Native neighbors. The report further noted that the furs passing through Detroit were being redirected to the English. In 1710, as a result of the report, Count Pontchartrain replaced

Cadillac by appointing him governor of Louisiana, a posting that Cadillac was very unhappy with. When Cadillac left the Great Lakes region, he was never to return.

In 1703, the fort was set on fire deliberately and partially destroyed. The exact cause of the fire and the culprit were never determined. In 1712, the fort was again partially destroyed by fire. This time, the cause was blazing arrows from a Native American attack. In 1718, the fort was completely renovated, making it one of the strongest posts in the Great Lakes region. In 1749, with new immigrants arriving from France, the stockade had to be enlarged. Additional troops arrived in 1751, and from this time on, the fort was called Fort Detroit, although the name was never formally changed.

On November 29, 1760, Fort Pontchartrain was surrendered to the English when they took control of New France and the Great Lakes region after the English capture of Montreal. The English enlarged Fort Pontchartrain and included about eighty houses outside the walls of the fort. Large bastions were built at each corner and over the two gates on the east and west sides. Blockhouses were also built for observation and defense.

As a common practice at the time, the gates were opened at sunrise and closed at sunset. Each of the large wooden gates had a small wicket gate that would allow a single person to pass through. The wickets were open until 9:00 p.m. If Natives entered to trade or for a council, their weapons were taken from them at the gate and returned to them when they left.

Six hundred miles away, the newly appointed British governor of Quebec, Jeffrey Amherst, introduced a number of new trading measures that would severely strain the relations between the British and their Native American trading partners in the Great Lakes region. Amherst forbade and made illegal the practice of gift giving. He ended the long-held practice of his traders visiting Native villages and ordered an end to providing the Natives with rum or other alcohol, along with very limited supplies of gunpowder and lead, which severely affected their ability to hunt (by this time many or most Natives no longer relied on the use of the bow and arrow).

In the spring of 1763, Chief Pontiac held a Native American war council a number of miles from Detroit. The plan was that Natives near each fort would wait for the first full moon of June and then strike each fort, killing all those who did not run away.

At Fort Pontchartrain on May 7, 1763, Pontiac and sixty Ottawa braves entered the fort with weapons concealed under blankets. The intent was to surprise the British soldiers of Fort Pontchartrain and the commander,

Major Henry Gladwin. The ruse did not surprise Major Gladwin, as he had been warned of the attack by a Native.

Pontiac withdrew from the fort with his 60 men and began to lay siege to the fort. The force of Ottawa, Huron, Potawatomi, and Wyandot braves grew from 60 to more than 400. On July 29, 1763, 260 British troops arrived at the fort under the command of Captain James Dalyell and tried to break up the siege. Pontiac sent a large force to ambush the British coming up the river, and the Battle of Bloody Run ended up costing the British nearly 60 men.

The British inside the fort continued to resist the siege, and by October, Pontiac was offering a truce, which Gladwin accepted. Most of the Natives returned to their villages to start the hunt for wintertime meat supplies. Pontiac lifted the siege on October 15 and moved south to the Maumee River.

In 1778, during the American Revolution, the English, fearing that Fort Pontchartrain would easily be taken over by the Americans, built Fort Lernoult, which was a stronger and larger fort, farther back from the Detroit River. Fort Pontchartrain was then abandoned and over the years completely dismantled, and the site waited for some new construction. While the territory on what is now the Michigan side of the Detroit River was ceded to the United States in the Treaty of Paris is 1783, the American government did not take control of the area until 1796.

The river flowing between Lake St. Clair and Lake Erie was named by Cadillac as Le Detroit du Lac Erie, meaning the "Strait of Lake Erie." Jerome Phelypeaux de Pontchartrain, the French secretary of the navy, approved a plan for a new fort and allowed Cadillac the funds to construct a new fur trading outpost.

On July 23, 1701, the Cadillac expedition arrived at what is now known as Grosse Ile. The following day, the expedition moved upriver several miles to a bluff overlooking the river at a narrow point. Construction on Fort Pontchartrain began the next day with the felling of many trees and the clearing of land. The first building was a chapel dedicated to Saint Anne, patron saint of New France.

At the end of the King's War in 1760, a few months after the British captured New France and Montreal, Fort Pontchartrain surrendered to a British contingent led by Major Robert Rogers, and Fort Pontchartrain officially became known as Fort Detroit.

The British had no real idea how to deal with the Native population and felt that honest trade with the Natives was beneath them. The new British governor failed to understand the basic diplomatic practice of gift giving. The governor ordered that all trade with Native people to be discontinued and that providing alcohol of any kind was strictly forbidden. He also limited the amount of gunpowder and lead that would be given to the Native tribes.

During the American Revolutionary War, Fort Detroit was used by the British as a staging area and for training purposes. At the start of the Revolution, Fort Detroit had a population of nearly 1,500 people, with a mixture of some 90 slaves whether black or Native.

Although Fort Detroit was fortified with a few thousand British troops, Fort Detroit played no significant role in the eventual outcome of the American Revolution.

News of the peace treaty between Britain and the United States reached Detroit on May 6, 1783, but British commander Lieutenant Colonel Arent de Peyester had received no orders to evacuate or turn over the fort to the Americans. Unofficially, Great Britain wanted to retain control of the fur trade.

Eventually, in 1796, the British departed Fort Detroit and Fort Mackinac. There is strong evidence that the British continued to provide Native tribes with alcohol well after the dates the British departed U.S. forts.

The final remains of Fort Pontchartrain were destroyed in the Detroit Great Fire of 1805. Hotel Pontchartrain, a 367-room hotel, was built on the original site of Fort Pontchartrain. The hotel became a Wyndham Hotel in 2021.

Fort Pontchartrain/Detroit. *Artist Norman Liljegren.*

Earlier, in 1907, the first Hotel Pontchartrain was built on Cadillac Square at Woodward Avenue. This hotel was later sold and demolished in 1920.

A Michigan Historical Commission marker for Fort Pontchartrain du Detroit was placed at the southwest corner of Washington Boulevard and Jefferson Avenue. Today, the city's traffic, on new streets, makes its way across the former paths, lands, and fields of Fort Pontchartrain once trod by Native Americans and early French explorers. The French era, in Michigan, has faded into yesteryear, and little thought is now given by those who hurry past the place where Cadillac's little stockade once stood on the Detroit River.

Fort Repentigny/Sault Ste. Marie

Sault Ste. Marie
1751–1762

Three thousand years ago, after the last of the glaciers receded, the future U.S. city of Sault Ste. Marie, Michigan, was dealt a winning hand thanks to the developing geography. Lake Superior and its eastern outlet had been raised about twenty-one feet. This culminated in the lowering of water levels in what would become known as Lake Michigan and Lake Huron. The connection between Lake Superior and Lake Huron would become known as the St. Mary's River, or "Riviere du Ste. Marie" as the French referred to it.

With Lake Superior being twenty-one feet higher than the river outlet, the water had to find its way over and through a series of rock and boulder rapids in order to reach the lower St. Mary's River. The rapids were shallow and treacherous. The French called it a "sault," meaning "shallow rapids" among other things. The name stuck, and the French added "Le Sault de Ste. Marie," meaning the "Falls of St. Mary."

It is not known who may have lived at the Sault before the Ojibwas, Ottawas, and the Potawatomis. When the Jesuit missionaries arrived in the middle of the sixteenth century, it had long been used as a gathering place for local tribes due to the abundance of whitefish and the location being ideal for encampments.

In 1668, a Jesuit mission was founded at the gathering spot on the St. Mary's River. It was established at this location to afford the French Jesuits the opportunity to minister to the spiritual needs of the Native Americans.

One year later, the mission was abandoned by the Jesuits due to Natives deserting the area for their seasonal hunts. The Jesuits returned to the old mission—strategically located at the portage around the rapids between Lake Superior and the St. Mary's River—and reopened it in 1751.

The French, having had a trading post located at the St. Mary's River rapids as early as 1670 and almost a monopoly of the fur trade in the Upper Lakes region, decided in 1751 to establish a more permanent post there. French King Louis XV had heard many reports that some of the Native American fur trappers were bypassing the mission at the Sault and taking their furs directly to the English because the English were offering less expensive goods in trade and sometimes additional brandy.

The king sent two men to the Sault to build a fort to protect the French fur trading interests in the Upper Midwest area of what he referred to as New France. The men, Captain Louis le Gardeur de Repentigny and Captain Louis de Bonne, were charged with building a small fort to be operated and maintained under the direction of De Repentigny.

In 1751, Captain De Repentigny and Captain De Bonne built a palisaded fort on the southern bank of the St. Mary's River just downstream from the rapids. The purpose was to protect the French fur trade in the Great Lakes area. Captain Repentigny and his men cut 1,100 wooden pickets and timber for three large houses over the winter to be erected in the spring. The fort was built as a 110-foot-square palisade that enclosed the four houses. Because the French military party had arrived in the early fall of 1751, the weather was so severe that work on the proposed fort had to be delayed. On October 10, the Sault was struck by a blizzard that dumped fifteen inches of snow before the storm ended. For the rest of the winter, the soldiers were ordered to continue cutting down the trees and preparing timber for the building of the fort and structures in the spring. Other buildings were added outside the fort later in the spring and summer of 1752.

The condition that the king laid down was that a fort be erected and maintained at the personal expense of De Repentigny and De Bonne and that all of the land composing the 225 square miles of the King's Proclamation be placed under cultivation. About 1,100 pickets 15 feet in length were prepared for a palisade and as the necessary material for the construction of three houses 30 feet long and 20 feet wide and two others each 25 feet long and 20 feet wide. The fort, when completed, enclosed a palisade 110 feet square with a redoubt of oak 12 feet square and reaching 12 feet in height.

Jean Baptiste Cadeau, a French trapper/trader, had married a Native woman from a local tribe. He was experienced at trading and spoke the local language. Cadeau was hired by De Repentigny to manage the fort and trading posts during his frequent absences. Cadeau was also placed in charge of a section of the grant of land for the purpose of inaugurating farming operations, and De Repentigny had also arranged for two slaves to work to cultivate his acres. Cadeau and his Ojibwa wife settled into the main house and carefully watched the clearing of the land. For whatever reason, Cadeau changed the spelling of his name to "Cadotte." Throughout all the Lake Superior district and far into the West, the Native Americans knew and trusted him and his sons.

De Repentigny's plans to develop his land into a valuable farm were temporarily disturbed when war between France and Great Britain broke out in 1754. Every son of France in the New World was needed to defend the colony. In 1755, De Repentigny fought at the head of a regiment of Canadians at Lake George. The next year found him again at Sault Ste. Marie directing the efforts of his handful of settlers. The British were rapidly getting a foothold on Quebec, then a stronghold in New France. Leaving Cadotte in command of the fort, De Repentigny left to fight alongside the governor of New France. The De Repentigny party arrived safely at the citadel, but not in time to make a difference. French rule in Canada was coming to an end. Those Native braves who returned to the fort at the Sault carried back with them the story of the Battle on the Plains of Abraham, but sadly De Repentigny did not return.

Cadotte waited patiently, watching for his commander's return, but one day there was sighted coming up the river a flotilla of canoes bearing a detachment of British soldiers under Lieutenant Jemette. They landed and in the name of the British king took possession of the post. In 1760, the fort was captured by the British and held by them until it was destroyed by fire and abandoned on December 22, 1762.

Legend has it that during the skirmish between the English and French, Cadotte, loyal to the French, defied the British troops all alone until he was shot, although he did survive his wounds. The very next year, he entered into a partnership with British trader Alexander Henry, who was to be one of the few survivors of the massacre at Fort Michilimackinac in the spring of 1763, known as the "Conspiracy of Pontiac."

In 1825, the De Bonne descendants began to press their claims to what had by then become very valuable land. They were joined within a few years by the De Repentigny heirs, some of whom were living in poverty in the Caribbean. After several disappointing legal attempts, they obtained passage of a special bill by the U.S. Senate in 1860 authorizing the federal district

Fort Repentigny/Sault Ste. Marie. *Artist Norman Liljegren.*

court in Michigan to decide the validity of their claim. The court ruled in their favor in 1861, but the U.S. Supreme Court reversed the federal court's decision in 1867, citing the lapse of time and the failure of the original grantees to improve the land as its primary reason. Thus ended the last claim to Michigan lands that had once been under French occupation and ownership.

Fort Saginaw

Saginaw
1822–1824

The area of the present city of Saginaw was inhabited from about 1000 BC to AD 1000 by Hopewell Woodland groups, followed by the Anishinaabes. Some historians believe that the Sauk people at one time lived in the area and were driven out by Ojibwas (Chippewas) before the area was first visited by Europeans.

French missionaries and traders first appeared in the area during the late seventeenth century. A trading post was established by Louis Campau in 1816. Campau also platted the "town" area, but early on very few lots were ever sold.

The Treaty of Saginaw in 1819 cleared the way for European settlement. In 1822, the U.S. government established the territorial county of Saginaw and sent the military in to build Fort Saginaw in an effort to control the Ojibwas in the region. The mosquito infestation and oppressive humidity in the Saginaw Valley region were severe, making the fort almost uninhabitable. The first and only commander at Fort Saginaw was Major Daniel Baker.

On July 22, 1822, along the banks of the Saginaw River, Major Baker selected the building site for Fort Saginaw. The site that Baker selected for the fort was on a bluff on the west bank of the Saginaw River. He wrote that he picked the place, "below the forks of the river opposite Riley's reservation and adjoining the place known in this country by the name of the trading establishment," because of its defensible location and its proximity to water and timber. Baker established a thirty- or forty-acre military reservation, and his men began work on the fort immediately. We do not know precisely where the fort was situated, but based on observations provided by early American settlers in Saginaw, we can guess that it was located on the high ground adjacent to the river, approximately where Court Street intersects with Hamilton Street. The former parade ground is still a city greenspace today, Bouchard Park and the Courthouse Square, both along North Michigan Avenue.

The Saginaw Valley region includes an extensive network of many rivers and streams that converge into the Saginaw River and provided a means for easy travel for the Native American population among numerous settlements and hunting areas, as well as access to Lake Huron. The name "Saginaw" most likely comes from the Ojibwa words meaning "place of the outlet" (*sag*, or "opening," and *ong*, or "place of").

French missionaries first reached the area in the seventeenth century. Henri Nouvel, a Jesuit missionary who made repeated visits to the Native Americans present in the area, is of particular significance. He recorded information concerning his travels during the 1670s in his journals. The French controlled the territory consisting of the present-day state of Michigan until it was ceded to the British following the Seven Years' War in 1763. The French established permanent settlements in many locations throughout the Great Lakes, but most of the interior of the Lower Peninsula of Michigan, including the Saginaw River Valley, was undeveloped. Both the French and the British primarily maintained settlements for trade and strategic defense, neither of which provided much reason to develop the Saginaw region.

Following the British defeat during the American Revolutionary War, Michigan was officially ceded by treaty to the United States in 1784. Despite this, the British remained in de facto control of the territory for long after. It was not until the conclusion of the War of 1812 that all presence of British military was removed from what is present-day Michigan.

In 1823, nearly the entire garrison was disabled by malaria caused by horrendous swarms of mosquitoes. Dr. Zina Pitcher, the post surgeon, did everything he could do to make the men as comfortable as possible. Dr. Pitcher also fell victim himself. At one point, he was so ill that he had to be carried on a litter to see his patients. Many of the troops died from malaria. As a result, the fort was abandoned in 1824, and the remaining troops were reassigned to Detroit.

This incident led Major Baker to make the statement that "only Natives, muskrats and bullfrogs can live in Michigan." This statement, in a formal report, was sent to Washington, D.C., and was one more obstacle that Michigan Territorial Governor William Cass had to overcome in his attempt to argue for Michigan statehood.

We do not know what the actual fort looked like, although it was most likely to have been made of vertical posts lashed together, with redoubts in opposing corners. Fort Saginaw was one of many forts that the U.S. government built immediately following the War of 1812 and was comparatively modest. A simple wooden palisade 200 feet wide by 350 feet long surrounded these buildings.

The short-lived fort was abandoned in 1824. No records of Fort Saginaw's construction describing the size, shape, or footprint of the fort are known to exist. Archaeological evidence is scanty, and the full story of Fort Saginaw as one of the most obscure forts in Michigan remains a mystery.

Fort St. Joseph, Niles

Niles
1691–1795

In 1684, a small spot of land near present-day Niles, Michigan, was given to the Jesuits by the French king in order to build a mission. In 1691, Fort St. Joseph was built next to the mission by Augustin le Gardeur de

Courtemanche. It was located on the banks of the St. Joseph River, about twenty-five miles east of where the river empties into Lake Michigan.

Fort St. Joseph, built in the palisaded style, contained only a few buildings. The location of the fort had strategic importance but not great military importance. Its location near where two main Indian trails crossed was a major consideration, as these were the principal trade and war routes in southern Michigan. Europe's growing demand for animal fur pushed traders to the area of the fort, and the fort was used as a trading post for the French and Native Americans.

French Jesuit priests became a fairly prevalent sight in and around the St. Joseph River basin during the seventeenth and eighteenth centuries, building missions all over the Great Lakes region that would later become trading hubs. The main mission of the Society of Jesus missionaries was to travel to Indian villages and attempt to convert Natives to Christianity. For the Jesuits, the trading of furs was only a secondary consideration.

Fort St. Joseph was fairly small, with about fifteen houses in and around the fort accommodating the enlisted men and officers. There was also a blacksmith and an interpreter. The fort did not hold great military value, other than for watching the fur trade and maintaining peace in the area. Few Europeans wanted to live in the area because it was still quite harsh and underdeveloped. Fort St. Joseph formed the backbone of the French fur trade.

Fur clothing had become very fashionable in Europe in the sixteenth century. A nice fur hat and coat were symbols of wealth and status. French traders relied on Native Americans to get the furs and trade them for European goods, such as muskets, knives, and kettles; they also developed a taste for alcohol. The French, for the most part, treated Native Americans with respect, sometimes giving them extra gifts to help build relationships. Forts like St. Joseph became hubs for commerce.

For three years, life at the fort was peaceful, but in the spring of 1694, an Iroquois war party attacked the fort. Courtemanche and his troops defended the fort so vigorously that the Indians withdrew and gave up further attempts to destroy it.

After the French and Indian War, Fort St. Joseph and other French forts were handed over to the British. On November 19, 1761, British Ensign Francis Schlosser arrived at Fort St. Joseph and took command of the garrison.

On May 25, 1763, a band of Potawatomis arrived from Detroit and asked for a council with Schlosser. Unaware of Chief Pontiac's plan to rid the

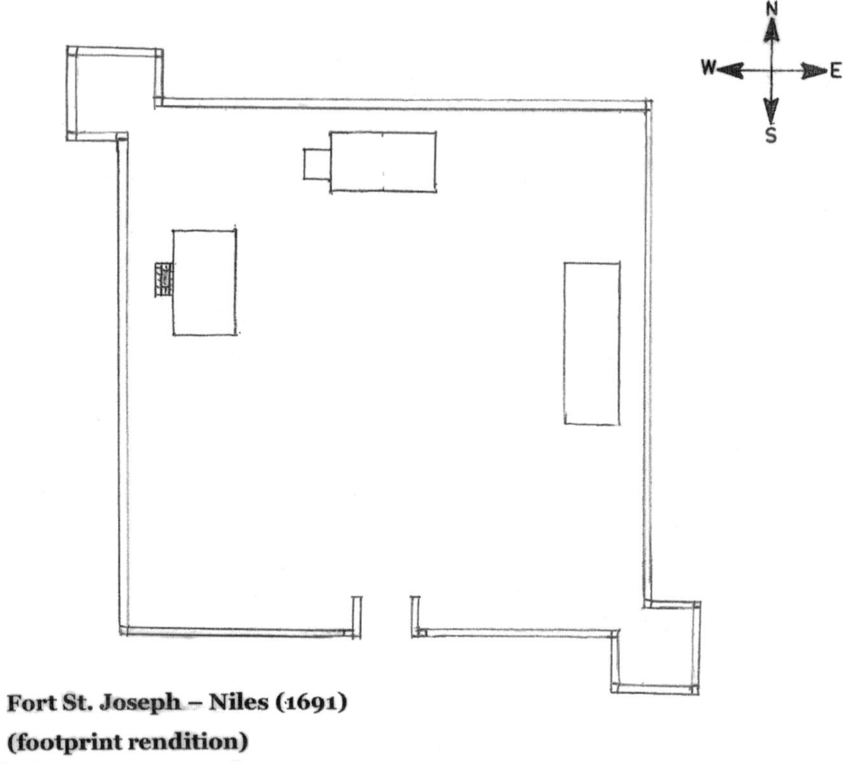

Fort St. Joseph, Niles (footprint rendering). *Courtesy of author.*

territory of all English people, Schlosser had no suspicion of danger. As the Natives entered his quarters, Schlosser heard a war whoop and shots from the direction of the barracks.

Schlosser was seized by the Natives during the attack, in which nine soldiers were killed. Schlosser and the six surviving soldiers were then taken to Detroit and exchanged for Native prisoners.

Fort St. Joseph was never abandoned; however, the trading activity was considerably slower. But within a year, the trading post again became a busy hub for French fur traders..

In early 1781, a group of French and Native Americans, looking for an alliance and to avenge English grievances in the area, approached Spanish Governor Francisco Cruzat in St. Louis, asking for his help to attack Fort St. Joseph. The governor, wanting to reduce the amount of British control in the region, gave his consent and financial support. The detachment was successful, and a Spanish flag was raised over Fort St. Joseph. The next day, the victors left the fort. This is why Niles, Michigan, claims to be the "City of Four Flags," as the area was occupied by France, England, Spain, and the United States.

Within a few weeks of the Spanish leaving Fort St. Joseph, the British again controlled the territory, but the fort was never again fully garrisoned by military troops. The British maintained the fort until after the U.S. victory in the Northwest Indian War and the signing of the Jay Treaty in 1795, which settled the northern border. After the British abandoned Fort St. Joseph, it fell into ruin and was overtaken by forest.

The fort site was not rediscovered until 1998. An archaeology excavation has been underway since 2002. Among the rare artifacts discovered is an intact Jesuit religious medallion from the 1730s, one of only two ever found in North America. In December 2010, the team revealed a foundation wall and corner posts of one of the original buildings. Archaeological digs, conducted by staff professionals from Western Michigan University, are an ongoing seasonal operation. The site is listed in the National Register of Historic Places and is also a state-registered site.

Fort St. Joseph, Port Huron

Port Huron

1686–1689

The French successfully established colonies in the Caribbean in the sixteenth century. Those early colonies supplied the motherland with sugar and other agricultural products. The French were less successful with their northern colonies. The early settlers in Canada found it difficult to raise food crops and did not have the skills the Native Americans had of supporting themselves from their environment. They depended on shipments from France. Furthermore, the Iroquois frequently attacked the small French villages and settlements. New France was a dangerous place for the few French settlers who tried to survive there in the 1600s.

The French population of Canada grew slowly. French governmental officials and the military wished to secure the land for France and prevent the English, the Spanish, or any other nation from evicting them.

Priests from France wanted to convert the Native Americans to Roman Catholicism and French civilization. And then there were traders—many of them former soldiers—who wished to get rich by trading with the Natives for furs that they could sell at great profit in France.

Daniel Greysolon, Sieur DuLuth, was born in Saint-Germain-en-Laye in 1639 or 1640 and served in the French military. He rose to the rank of lieutenant in 1657 and was appointed a member of the King's Guard seven years later. Members of his family had immigrated to Canada and he joined them in New France in 1678. He quickly became an explorer, joining with members of the French military to explore the Upper Great Lakes region. He may have been the first European to reach the western end of Lake Superior, in 1679, and then went on to explore the upper plateau area north of the headwaters of the Mississippi River.

Daniel Greysolon was highly significant in the exploration of the Upper Great Lakes and the Midwest. In addition, he apparently was quite successful in building productive relationships between French settlers and the Native tribes who lived around Lake Superior. Apparently, he devoted much effort to trying to convince the various tribes to cease fighting with one another and trade with the French. Unlike the British, quite a few French administrators promoted peace with the Natives. The French missionaries, of course, wanted to convert the Natives, and the voyageurs wished to trade European products to Natives for the furs they supplied. Many French men, but few French women, came to the most remote areas of Canada, so many of the French traders and trappers formed families with Native women. Greysolon died in Montreal in 1710 and is an honored figure in Canadian history. The second-largest city in Minnesota and an interesting thoroughfare in Montreal bear his name, or at least an Anglicized version of his name: Duluth.

The French knew that they had two enemies they might need to fight in North America. The British had a presence on Hudson Bay to the north and had colonies along the Atlantic shoreline. In addition, the Iroquois still threatened the French. As he continued to travel throughout the Great Lakes region, Daniel Greysolon realized that the mouth of the St. Clair River would be an excellent location for a fort. Should the British try to pass through Lake St. Clair or Lake Huron, they could easily be stopped by French forces stationed at this key junction.

St. Ignace may have been the first location in Michigan where the French established a permanent settlement, but Fort St. Joseph was the second such location, although it was not to remain established for long.

In 1684, Daniel Greysolon, Sieur DuLuth, made peace between the fierce Sioux and other Michigan tribes, thus opening the west, beyond Lake Superior, to the French.

In 1686, Governor Denonville ordered DuLuth to build a fort between Lake Huron and Lake Erie to prevent the English traders from reaching the Upper Lakes. He chose a spot at the head of the St. Clair River, at the approximate location of the present-day site of what had been the Thomas Edison Inn but is now called the Double Tree Hotel, as well as the Thomas Edison Depot Museum, under the Blue Water Bridge in Port Huron.

With fifty men, he built a simple stockade and named it Fort St. Joseph. It was approximately 190 square feet without the bastions and was separated from the St. Clair River by about forty paces, near McNeil Creek, which at that time emptied into the St. Clair River but has long since dried up. This old streambed can been seen at Port Huron's Palmer Park, where it is used for ice skating and sledding in the winter.

The construction and location of the fort were necessary if the French were to retain control of the fur trade in the North and West. In the summer of 1687, Governor Denonville planned a campaign against the Iroquois, allies of the English, to punish them for guiding English traders into French territory. To augment his force, he ordered the leaders in the region to meet him at Lake Ontario. The leaders were to assemble their forces at Fort St. Joseph, which would become a mustering and mobilization center for nearly two hundred French troops and five hundred Native Americans. From there they would move on to Lake Ontario.

Henry de Tonty and Nicolas Perrot arrived with a contingent of soldiers and Indians, and La Durantaye arrived with English and Native prisoners. There was great rejoicing and merriment at the fort. Indians and Frenchmen celebrated the gathering with great enthusiasm. DuLuth and other leaders, wanting to avoid any wild demonstrations by the Natives, hurried them away from the fort for the rendezvous with Governor Denonville at Lake Ontario. On the way, they captured a party of English traders headed for Michilimackinac led by Major Patrick McGregory.

Governor Denonville's expedition against the Iroquois did not accomplish what he had hoped, but it did show how a large body of troops and Natives could be raised for the defense of New France. The Natives and former French soldiers did not see any military action, grew bored, and quickly moved back to their home territories when winter approached.

Louis Armand de Lon D'arce, Baron de LaHontan, was appointed as the new commander of Fort St. Joseph on September 14, 1687. LaHontan was an ardent sportsman and had a gifted ability as a writer. He enthusiastically described the Native American chase of the deer on the islands in the lower St. Clair River.

Hunting during the long winter, with little to do to pass the tedious days, LaHontan began to dream of a more populous place. In the spring of 1688, LaHontan had made a few attacks against the Iroquois tribes. In August, finding that his supplies were nearly gone and anticipating a negotiated peace to be made with the Iroquois, LaHontan decided that Fort St. Joseph was not worth maintaining and moved his troops to Fort Michilimackinac. It is not clear whether he simply abandoned the fort or if he burned it before he left.

In a document dating from 1690, measures for the improved defense of New France were recommended. The French stated that "it is well to preserve the posts we occupy in the country. They can be kept up at a very trifling expense and provide some measure of security for our fur traders."

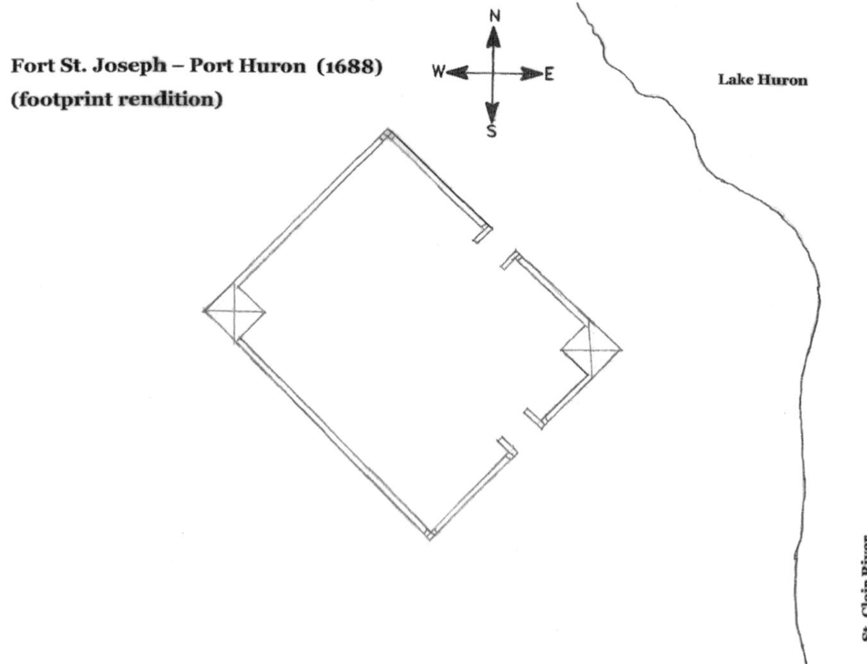

Fort St. Joseph, Port Huron (footprint rendering). *Courtesy of author.*

In 1694, at a conference between the French and Native Americans, the Straits of Detroit was spoken of as a fine rendezvous point. In 1700, another council was held between the French and four Native nations of the Ottawas, Hurons, Potawatomis, and the Mississaugas. It must be remembered that the word *detroit* at that time had no relation to the locality of the present-day city of Detroit, which was not founded until 1701. The word *detroit* actually represented the entire waterway from Lake Erie to Lake Huron, and these references make it probable that there was a continuance of Fort St. Joseph until at least 1700.

Louis Armand de Lon D'arce, Baron de LaHontan, commanded Fort St. Joseph in 1688. Apparently he did not share Daniel Greysolon's idea about the importance of this location, so he abandoned this fort and moved to Fort DuBuade at St. Ignace with his forces. This ended the first permanent French settlement at present-day Port Huron.

This Fort St. Joseph had a brief recorded history, but its location is certain. In the book *New Voyages to North America*, LaHontan marked it clearly on his map, on the west bank at the head of the St. Clair River. This fort was sometimes referred to as Fort Detroit or Fort DuLuth. The mix-up in location is probably due to ignorance of LaHontan's map and to the fact that the word *detroit* was used to refer to both the St. Clair River and Detroit River.

After LaHontan's departure in 1689, the fort grounds eventually became overgrown with bushes and trees, and its physical existence slowly vanished. An archaeological dig on the site has produced a number of artifacts that are on display at the Port Huron Museum of Arts and History.

The strategic importance of this Fort St. Joseph site proved itself again when Captain Charles Gratiot established Fort Gratiot in 1814 almost on the same site chosen by the French 128 years earlier.

Fort Sinclair

St. Clair

1765–1814

In 1763, shortly after the "Conspiracy of Pontiac," British Lieutenant Patrick Sinclair arrived in Detroit and was placed in command of transporting the supplies between Detroit and Fort Michilimackinac, the two most important military posts on the Upper Great Lakes at the time. The route between the two posts could be very dangerous. While acting in that capacity, he was given orders by Colonel John Bradstreet, commander of Fort Detroit, to construct a small fort where the Pine River empties into the St. Clair River. Drawn by the natural beauty of the St. Clair Flats area, Sinclair obtained a deed in 1764 from the local Native American tribe for the British Crown. It was for a tract of land of about twenty-four thousand acres. He was also looking out for himself, obtaining a second deed with the local Native tribe for four thousand acres on which most of today's city of St. Clair now sits.

Patrick Sinclair was born in Lybster, Scotland, in 1736. He joined the Second Battalion of the Forty-Second Royal Highland Regiment in 1758. Britain and France were at time involved in the Seven Years' War, and Sinclair was sent to fight in the Caribbean. In 1761, Sinclair found himself serving on Lake Ontario and Lake Erie transporting men and supplies to distant British outposts. Then, in 1763, he was reassigned to Fort Detroit.

In 1765, Lieutenant Sinclair got busy, quickly building a vertical log fortification, a lumber mill, and a gristmill. He started the beginnings of a farm and an orchard, in addition to the house he built for his dream of developing a wilderness estate, which he would refer to as "the Pinery." Lieutenant Sinclair stayed in command of the fort until 1769, when he was ordered to back to England. The house Sinclair built at Fort Sinclair stayed in constant use until the mid-1800s and was referred to as the "Big House."

Fort Sinclair was built at the south side of the Pine River, approximately where the Cargill Salt Company stands today. With the approval of Colonel Bradstreet, Lieutenant Sinclair built a fort and named it in his own honor. He did not feel that he was being pretentious about this, as the fort was built almost entirely at his own expense and it was traditional for a fort to take the name of the builder. It was a large military and trading post consisting of earthworks, two barracks, two blockhouses, a rally post, and a wharf, all enclosed in a stockade mounted with a number of cannons.

Sinclair left his beloved Pinery in 1769 and sadly was never to return due to military obligations. He did appoint various agents to look after the Pinery. One agent, working with Sinclair at the time, was Francis Bellecour, whose daughter Mary Magdalene was born in the Pinery in 1774. Her birth is the first recorded birth at the small settlement. Old records indicate that the Pinery trading post continued to do good business for many years. Lumber from the Pinery was rafted down to Detroit, and the Sinclair estate continued to prosper. In 1780, Sinclair sent Jean Baptiste Point du Sable to replace the retiring Bellecour as his agent at the Pinery. Today, Du Sable is well known as the founder of Chicago. He managed the Pinery estate until 1784.

The British military lost interest in Fort Sinclair and pulled all the troops out in 1782. However, the trading post remained and prospered for many more years. The fort was continuously used by traders and for shelter until well after the War of 1812. As with most building made from material of the natural environment, it eventually fell into disrepair, rotted, and disappeared.

The purpose of the fort was to stop the hostilities between the British and the Natives. The hostilities were a direct result of France surrendering its North American territory to the British.

During the build-up of the Pinery, Sinclair erected a sawmill about four miles upstream on the Pine River, and under his direction, the land was cleared, houses were built, and orchards were planted. He created for himself "la manor" in size befitting an English duke.

Although there would seem to be a connection between the name Sinclair and the name of the modern city of St. Clair, there is no evidence to suggest that the city was named for Patrick Sinclair.

Nothing is known of Fort Sinclair's form or actual size, but it contained at least one brick building, portions of which were still standing in 1830. The fort was used for military purposes for only seven years, until about the time the United States took possession of the territory, although it did function as a trading post for another seventeen years. The fort never saw any military action, other than the regular military exercises conducted by the commander. Fort Sinclair did not figure into the security of the territory or the guardianship of the waterways. The old fort just gradually fell into decay and disappeared.

Fort Sinclair was a fortified fort in the strict sense of the word and did have a small garrison of troops, but a hostile shot was probably never fired from it or at it.

Historically, interest in the fort on the local level has been kept alive with the celebration of the "Feast of the Ste. Claire," cosponsored with the City of Port Huron every Memorial Day weekend.

With its large sawmill operation, the Pinery property formed the nucleus of the first great estate in Michigan and was a continuous settlement from the year 1764 to what today is the city of St. Clair.

WAYNE STOCKADE

Monroe County
1805–1813

One of the most interesting historical markers in Monroe County is at what today is the corner of East Elm Avenue and North Monroe Street in the city of Monroe. It is one of the most heavily traveled intersections in the area and also one that defines the earliest history of Monroe.

In 1805, the Wayne Stockade was built and holds the cherished position of being the first U.S. military post on Michigan soil to fly the American flag.

The stockade was built as a southern point of defense and logistics for the U.S. troops assigned to it. The logistics were important, given its location next to the River Raisin and Hull's Trace. This position provided both land and water access for the arrival of all the necessary munitions and supplies needed by the troops. To prepare for the almost certainty of another war with Britain, the soldiers at the Wayne Stockade built additional blockhouses for their quarters.

In August 1812, Captain Henry Brush was sent to Ohio to take control of a load of provisions. This assignment ended up requiring Captain Brush to build a new corduroy road, as the existing road was impassable for heavy wagons. As Captain Brush and his troops traveled back to Michigan, they were met at Urbana, Ohio, by a group of two hundred Ohio troops, who joined the group to make the journey back to Michigan.

Three times the Brush troops tried to push past the River Raisin, but they were repelled by British soldiers and Shawnees commanded by Tecumseh. After a second failed attempt to push past the River Raisin and the British troops, Captain Brush sent word to General Hull that he was outnumbered. But he was determined not to let the British get control of all the wagonloads of provisions being protected by his troops. Major Thomas Van Horne was dispatched by General Hull to assist Captain Brush. In the last battle, British Major Muir was wounded, and Tecumseh received wounds that would lead to his death. Unable to get to the Wayne Stockade, Brush, his men, and all the provisions they carried returned to Ohio, as they did not believe that General Hull could have made the decision to surrender.

All the troops in the Michigan Territory, including Brush's, were included in the terms of surrender. The next day, British Captain Elliot accompanied by a Wyandot Native and a Frenchman, reached Frenchtown and approached

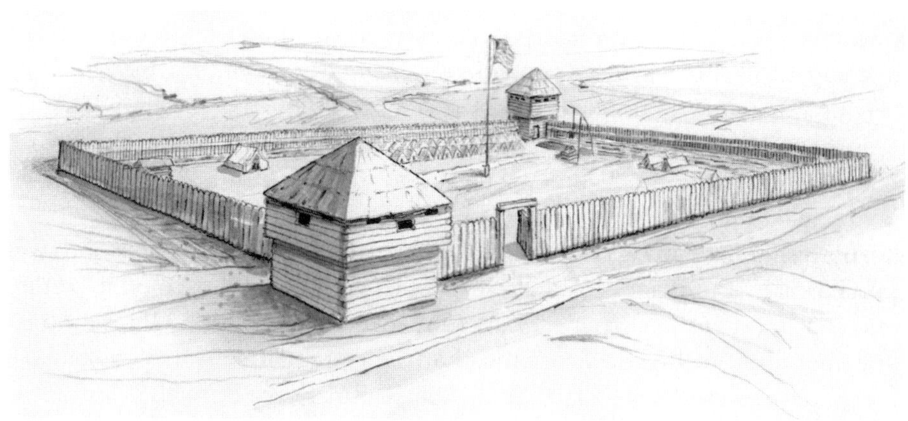

Top: Wayne Stockade. *Norman Liljegren, artist.*

Bottom: Wayne Stockade, Monroe, Michigan. *Fran Maedel, artist; courtesy of Connie Maedel-Diehl.*

the stockade. When the British officer made contact, he was blindfolded and brought into the stockade.

Captain Brush refused to accept that General Hull had surrendered, accusing Elliot of being a spy and placing him under arrest. The next day, some of the Michigan Militia who had been present at the surrender made it to Frenchtown and verified the surrender. Instead of complying with the terms, Brush and his men immediately headed deep into Ohio territory, leaving the helpless Elliot bound in the stockade.

Prior to the first Battle of Frenchtown on January 22, 1813, the British burned the Wayne Stockade to the ground to prevent the Americans from being able to use it.

After the war, the acre of land where the stockade once stood was purchased by the Honorable Charles Noble, who built a house on it. Today, one can stand at the corner of East Elm Avenue and North Monroe Street and imagine the Wayne Stockade that once stood there. Two associated blockhouses were located farther up the Raisin River from the site of the Wayne Stockade and near the mouth of Otter Creek. Both were burned down by the British in August 1812.

Part V

FORTS BUILT AFTER 1837

Fort Brady 2nd

Sault Ste. Marie
1893–1937

After the War of 1812 ended and the Treaty of Paris was signed with Great Britain, the Falls of the Saint Mary's River were left unoccupied, controlled by the British garrison stationed on Drummond Island. General Hugh Brady moved his troops from Sackett's Harbor to Sault Ste. Marie in 1822 to construct a stockade and barracks on the land ceded by the treaty of 1820 with the Chippewas. Brady first took over the former Nolin house and began the erection of a stockade, with blockhouses at the southwest and northeast corners. Pickets twelve feet high set four feet into the ground enclosed the principal buildings of the post in a solid stockade. Fort Brady was completed before the close of 1822 and stood on that location until 1892, when the detachment was moved to the top of Ashmun Hill.

The first Fort Brady was very important in the life of Sault Ste. Marie, occupying 26.14 acres extending 550 feet along the bank of the river and running parallel to Portage Street. The fort had a large garden, a cemetery, and a grove of large trees lying south of Portage Street. The main entrance was located on Portage Street, where a sentry with a rifle would pace back and forth. Just inside the entrance and to the right were long piles of cordwood used for heating the fort buildings because little if any coal was used for heating. On holidays, people would gather to watch the soldiers parade down Portage Street. The cannons would be fired and bugle calls made at random. Every spring, activities were held at the fort, including footraces, horse races, dog races, and canoe races. The races would take place on Water Street and at the base of the Saint Mary's River, starting at Sugar Island. Native American men frequently defeated American soldiers in canoe races.

The federal government realized that Sault Ste. Marie was an open target for sabotage and was a possible place to stage an invasion into the country and in 1866 ordered federal troops to occupy the post and return it to active duty. The fort buildings were reconstructed and remodeled. The federal troops were stationed here to protect the state locks and canals.

The decision to construct Fort Brady 2nd was made on August 26, 1852, granting land to the State of Michigan. The land consisted of the right of way through the Fort Brady military reservation and seventy-five thousand acres of land to build the Weitzel Lock and Canal. The canal was to be 100 feet wide and 12 feet deep and the lock 60 feet wide and 250 feet long, with a depth of 12 feet. The lock and canal would be defended by the National Guard and monitored by Fort Brady on the hilltop.

The Fort Brady garrison was moved to Ashmun Hill in the late 1880s and early 1890s. The construction began in 1892 and lasted through the turn of the century. In 1893, a public auction was held for the Old Fort Brady Military Reservation. The sale included sixty-two building lots and the greater part of the reservation. The government wanted cash and would give the fort to the highest bidder. Before the auction started, an auction sale sheet was handed out that contained a map of the sites for sale and a description sheet.

In 1894, Fort Mackinac was closed, and Fort Brady became the only fort in northern Michigan still in operation. The soldiers and supplies from Mackinac were diverted to Sault Ste. Marie.

In 1892, the U.S. government moved the garrison from the riverfront location to a new Fort Brady (2nd) on a hill overlooking the Soo Locks at a site chosen by General Phil Sheridan. After the U.S. removal of the garrison to the new fort in 1892–93, the old fort grounds were platted by Assistant Quartermaster George S. Hoyt. The growing city quickly covered over the remains of the old Fort Brady. Grave sites in the old fort cemetery were exhumed, and remains were reburied at another location.

Fort Brady 2nd was decommissioned in 1937 and would later house the Sault branch of Michigan Technological University. Many of the brick buildings from Fort Brady 2nd have been renovated and are still in use today as administrative and classroom buildings and dormitories as part of Lake Superior State University.

FORT WAYNE

Detroit

1848–1971

Although Fort Wayne was not constructed prior to Michigan statehood in 1837, it is important to acknowledge the requirements that led to its construction with the events of the period. Fort Wayne is located in the city of Detroit at the foot of Livernois Avenue in the old Delray neighborhood on the Detroit River. The original 1848 limestone barracks (with later brick additions) still stands, as does the 1845 star fortification (renovated in 1863 with brick exterior facing). On the fort grounds, but outside the original star fort, are additional barracks, officers' quarters, a hospital, shops, a recreation building, a commissary, ga uardhouse, a garage, and stables.

The fort sits on ninety-six acres. In the 1970s, eighty-three acres, including the original star fort and a number of buildings, were operated by the City of Detroit as a historic museum. The remaining area was operated by the U.S. Army Corp of Engineers as a boatyard. The fort was designated a Michigan State Historic Site in 1958 and listed in the National Register of Historic Places in 1971.

The site Fort Wayne is built on has a history going back to about the year AD 1000. About nineteen Native American burial mounds were present in the immediate area, as well as a larger one at the mouth of the Rouge River. The sole remaining burial mound at Fort Wayne was excavated by archaeologists from the University of Michigan in the early twentieth century and at that time was found to contain human remains more than nine hundred years old. A type of pottery found there is unique to the site—it was subsequently dubbed "Wayne Ware." The present star fort was built atop one of the burial mounds. The site originally consisted of a high sand mound, with freshwater springs found along the marshy waterfront of the Detroit River.

When Cadillac built Fort Pontchartrain, thereby founding the future city of Detroit, he also purportedly made arrangements with the local Potawatomi people to set up a small village at the future site of Fort Wayne for purposes of trading; this was occupied and thriving by 1710.

The opening shots of the War of 1812 were fired in the vicinity of Fort Wayne's future site, although war had not been officially declared yet. Michigan militiamen bombarded the town of Sandwich, Canada (later annexed into Windsor), on July 4, 1812. Later in the course of the War of 1812, British General Isaac Brock crossed the narrowest part of the Detroit River with his troops and landed on the future Fort Wayne site before marching to Detroit. In the ensuing Siege of Detroit, American General William Hull, believing himself completely surrounded and outnumbered, surrendered Fort Shelby to the British without offering any resistance. The British later abandoned the fort, and American troops reoccupied it. In 1815, the future Fort Wayne site was used for the signing of the Treaty of Springwells, which marked the official end of hostilities between the American government and the local Native American tribes of the area who had allied with the British during the war. Among those present for the signing of the treaty were Lewis Cass, a future Michigan governor, and General William Henry Harrison, a future U.S. president. Following the end of the war, Fort Shelby fell into disrepair, and in 1826, it was sold to the City of Detroit and demolished.

In the late 1830s, small, short-lived rebellions occurred in Canada to protest corruption in its colonial government. Many Americans believed that there was widespread Canadian support for these rebellions and formed volunteer militias to overthrow Canada's colonial government. This led to a series of militia attacks on Canada known as the Patriot War. However, at the same time, the U.S. government realized that there was a lack of fortifications along the northern border suitable to repel a potential British attack and, in particular, no counterpart to the British Fort Malden in Amherstburg. In 1841, Congress appropriated funds to build a chain of forts stretching from the East Coast to the Minnesota Territory, including one at Detroit.

Soon afterward, the U.S. Army sent Lieutenant Montgomery C. Meigs to Detroit. Meigs bought up riverfront farm property three miles below Detroit in today's Springwells Township. Construction on the fort began in 1842. The original fortifications were cedar-riveted earthen walls. The fort was completed in 1851, costing $150,000. The Army named the new fort for Revolutionary War hero General "Mad" Anthony Wayne, who had taken possession of Detroit from the British in 1796.

The original fort is star-patterned, with walls of earthen ramparts faced with cedar, covering vaulted brick tunnels that contain artillery ports.

The design was based on fortifications developed by Sebastian Vauban, a seventeenth-century French military engineer. Artillery emplacements atop the walls were designed for ten-inch cannons, mounted to fire over the parapet, although there is no indication that artillery intended for the fort was ever installed. There is a dry moat surrounding the fort.

Although the star fort today is substantially similar to the original construction, some changes have been made. Starting in 1863, under the supervision of Thomas J. Cram, the walls of the fort were reconstructed, replacing the original cedar facing with brick and concrete. In addition, the entranceway to the fort has been altered. The original entrance to the fort was a small sally port in the southeast bastion. In 1938, an arched entrance was constructed through the fort's walls to accommodate modern vehicular traffic; later, the arches were removed to fit larger trucks.

Within the star fort (and built at approximately the same time) is a three-and-a-half-story limestone troop barracks consisting of five independent but adjacent sections. Each section contains a ground-floor mess hall, two floors of barracks rooms, and an attic. Brick additions were added to the rear of the building in 1861 housing washrooms and kitchens. Next to the barracks is a powder magazine, also constructed of limestone. Additional buildings originally built within the star fort, such as officers' housing, have long since been destroyed.

Numerous additional buildings have been built on fort grounds outside of the star fort. A row of wooden Victorian-style officers' homes was built in the 1880s. In 1937, these homes were completely refurbished and clad in brick by WPA workers. One home was restored in the 1980s to its original appearance. A Spanish-American War guardhouse, built in 1889, is in the center of the fort grounds. The guardhouse was restored in 1984. In 1890, a brick hospital was built, with a later addition in 1898. In 1905, a new guardhouse, still in use today, was built near the gate to the fort grounds. Around the same time, four barracks buildings for enlisted men were built, as well as a service club (1903), headquarters (1905), and post office. By 1928, duplex-style housing for senior NCOs had been added. In 1939, more NCO houses were built in a row facing Jefferson Avenue.

Before any cannons had been installed at the newly constructed Fort Wayne, the United States and Britain peacefully resolved their differences, eliminating the need for a fort on the Detroit River. Fort Wayne remained unused for a decade after its initial construction, manned only by a single watchman. There is evidence suggesting that the fort was actually a final stop on the Underground Railroad during its dormant years. An Irish farmer who lived next to the fort operated a small ferry to Canada to supplement his income, the only such ferry in this part of the city at that time.

In 1861, the American Civil War again made Fort Wayne relevant. British sympathy for the Confederacy renewed fears of an attack from Canada, leading to a reconstruction and strengthening of the fort walls. Two weeks after the beginning of the war, the Michigan First Volunteer Infantry Regiment was mustered into service at Fort Wayne. For the rest of the Civil War, the fort served as a mustering center for troops from Michigan, as well as a place for veterans to recover from their wounds. Alfred Gibbs was the first commander to occupy the fort, having served his parole at Fort Wayne after being captured by the Confederacy.

After the Civil War and until 1920, Fort Wayne served as a garrison post, with regiments rotated from the western frontier for rest. In 1875, the City of Detroit annexed a portion of Springwells Township; in 1884, it annexed more of the township east of Livernois Avenue, including all land adjacent to Fort Wayne.

During the Spanish-American War, troops from the fort headed to Cuba and to the Philippines. The fort's guardhouse also housed the first telephone exchange in southwestern Detroit.

During the Great Depression, Fort Wayne was opened to homeless families and housed workers in the Civilian Conservation Corps.

During World War I, Fort Wayne became instrumental in the acquisition of cars, trucks, and spare parts for the military. This motor vehicle supply function reached its peak in World War II, when Fort Wayne was designated a motor supply depot and additional buildings were constructed for warehousing and shipping. At that time, Fort Wayne was the largest motor supply depot in the entire world, with the command center controlling the flow of materiel from the automobile factories to the citywide network of storage and staging facilities, which included the Michigan State Fairgrounds and the Port of Detroit terminal. Every single tank, truck, jeep, tire, or spare part that was sent to the fronts of World War II from the Detroit factories came through Fort Wayne. At that time, there was a railroad spur along the riverfront and docks for large ships, and more than two thousand (mostly civilian women) workers were employed. Fort Wayne served as home to Italian POWs captured during the North African campaign and were employed as servants, cooks, and janitors. After Italy's surrender, the POWs were given the chance to return to Italy, but many chose to remain and settle in Detroit.

At the end of World War II, plans were made to close the fort. In 1948, the star fort and original barracks were turned over to the City of Detroit's historical commission for operation as a military museum. In the 1950s, anti-aircraft guns were installed at the fort, later upgraded to Nike-Ajax missiles. During the Cold War, Fort Wayne served as an entrance station for the armed services, with thousands of enlistees and draftees being sworn in during the Korean War and Vietnam War. The fort was again used to provide housing to displaced families after the 1967 12th Street riot, with the last families staying at the fort until 1971.

The remainder of Fort Wayne was turned over piecemeal to the City of Detroit, with the last bit of property delivered in 1976. Over the years, hundreds of thousands of young Michigan men and women began their military careers inside the walls of Fort Wayne, mustering out to the various services, various locations, and various foreign wars.

From 1949 until 2006, the Fort Wayne Military Museum was operated by the Detroit Historical Museum. Since early 2006, the fort has been operated by the Detroit Recreation Department, assisted by the Historic Fort Wayne Coalition, the Friends of Fort Wayne, and the Detroit Historical Society.

Also on the grounds are the Tuskegee Airmen Museum and an ancient Indian burial mound.

Fort Wilkins

Copper Harbor
1844–1870

Fort Wilkins also falls into the category of forts built after Michigan statehood that had critical requirements for the security of upper Michigan. In the early 1840s, a copper rush took place, with fortune-seekers moving from all directions to the peninsula. The U.S. government was concerned about possible disorder and violence, and lake shipping interests asked the government to build an aid to navigation so that essential supplies could be shipped in and the copper moved out.

Copper Harbor is located at the northern tip of the Keweenaw Peninsula, bordering Lake Superior. It is one of the best natural harbors in Keweenaw County and was a quick focus of attention after copper was discovered on the peninsula in the 1830s.

The U.S. Army occupied Fort Wilkins, located east of Copper Harbor, Michigan, on the strait of land between Copper Harbor and the northern shore of Lake Fanny Hooe, in 1844. The troops stationed there were intended to help with local law enforcement and keep the peace between miners and the local Ojibwas, some of whom opposed the Treaty of La Pointe, which had ceded the area to the United States in 1842–43.

However, the fort proved to be unnecessary. The Ojibwas largely accepted the influx, and the miners were law-abiding. The U.S. Army built twenty-seven structures—including a guardhouse, powder magazine, seven officers' quarters, two barracks, two mess halls, hospital, storehouse, sutler's store, quartermaster's store, bakery, blacksmith's shop, carpenter's shop, icehouse, four quarters for married enlisted men, stables, and a slaughterhouse—to house the operations of two full-strength infantry companies. Several of these structures still survive. Others have been rebuilt following archaeological excavations.

When it was first garrisoned in 1844, two companies (A and B of the Fifth Infantry) were stationed there. When war was declared with Mexico, the soldiers were needed elsewhere. Companies A and B were sent to Texas and were replaced by Company K. The next year, Company K was also sent to Mexico, and in 1846, the fort was temporarily abandoned, leaving behind a single caretaker, Sergeant William Wright.

After the passing of Wright in 1855, the fort was subsequently rented by a Dr. Livermore, who hoped to open a health resort for people to come and take the bracing lake air. This plan fell through after his death in 1861. Dr. Livermore's tombstone and that of his daughter can still be found at the Copper Harbor Cemetery.

After the Civil War, the U.S. Army reoccupied Fort Wilkins for a few years in 1867–70. The Army needed a place for men to serve out the rest of their enlistments from the war. Company E was stationed there from 1867 until May 1869, when it was replaced by Company K, First Infantry. The Army permanently abandoned the facility at the end of August 1870.

In 1848, the Copper Harbor Lighthouse complex was established on the tip of the eastern point of land, also sometimes called Hays Point, which sits at the entrance of the harbor. In 1923, the fort and adjacent lighthouse became a Michigan state park.

The historic portion of Fort Wilkins and nearby lighthouse are operated as a unit of the Michigan Department of Natural Resources and Environmental Park and Recreation Division, as is the adjacent state park. As of 2010, the facility is open to the public in the summer months. For ten weeks each summer (June through August), the fort is staffed with costumed personnel; they are historical interpreters portraying Army life during the fort's final summer as an active post.

Part VI

THE MICHIGAN FUR TRADE

For the Europeans, the fur trade in Michigan and the entire Upper Midwest began with the French. Starting in the early 1600s and lasting for almost two hundred years, the business life of Michigan was centered on the trading of furs—first between the French and Native American tribes and then including the British, the Americans, and, to a lesser extent, the Spanish.

The fur trade had a strong impact on the lives of Native Americans starting in the early seventeenth century, ultimately ending in what can be considered a predictable way in the late nineteenth century. As skilled hunters and trappers, Native Americans were enlisted to be trading partners, which in the beginning was very lucrative for local tribes. But as time went on, the tribes were exposed to more white culture, and their exposure to European diseases that their bodies could not fight against left the Native tribes with battles that they could not win.

In exchange for their fur pelts, Natives received European goods along with firearms and liquor. The alcohol would prove to be the most devastating and long-lasting element of the contact between the Europeans and the Native Americans. The trade goods at first improved the tribes' lives and economy, along with their military strength, but eventually they made many of them dependent on receiving European goods.

Early on in the French fur trade, the principal markets were Sault Ste. Marie, the Mackinac straits area, and Detroit. To expand farther into the Upper Midwest, the French made trade pacts with Native American tribes.

The tribes had experienced hunters and trappers with the skills to cover a much more expansive area.

The European market for fur was ravenous. Beyond the highly prized beaver fur, Native Americans also collected and traded the pelts of deer, pine marten, raccoon, fox, mink, otter, and muskrat. In exchange, the Natives received iron hatchets, knives, cooking pots, traps, needles, and fishhooks, along with wool blankets and beads for making jewelry and decorative items.

New France, centered in Montreal, issued trading licenses, which were inexpensive but required the European trader to conduct business in a manner that many thought gave the government too much of the profit. This situation led a great many unlicensed traders into the woods hoping to cash in on the wealth of unregulated trade areas and Native American partners.

Many of these unlicensed French traders took Native American wives, creating the mixed offspring called Métis, who would later play a major role in maintaining good relations between Native American tribes and the traders, specifically the French.

The second result from trade with the Europeans was the long-term ecological effect of disrupting the balance of nature by depleting the source of fur-bearing animals.

Early on, the French thoroughly exploited the fur trade, which was the ultimate determining factor in the French expansion into the Upper Midwest. For the fur trade, starting with Jacques Cartier in 1534 along the St. Lawrence River, the original intent was to find a passageway to the Orient. What he found instead was an untapped source of high-quality furs and Native Americans eager to trade them for European goods.

Samuel de Champlain arrived in New France in 1603 with the express purpose of exploring the northern woods and trading with the Natives. He traded with all the eastern Canadian tribes, which turned into huge profits, but it was the Hurons, living farther to the west, who became the most bountiful suppliers. From 1616 to 1650, Champlain developed a trading empire with the Native tribes from the western Great Lakes to the Hudson Bay to the St. Lawrence River.

A trader was an agent who dealt with the local Native tribes. The trader had to be a shrewd negotiator and needed to have the ability to communicate with tribes even when the language was not clearly understood. These traders had to be rough, strong men who could paddle a canoe for hours and carry heavy packs of furs over the many portages. (A portage is the act of carrying the canoe and all equipment over a relatively short dry section of land between two bodies of navigable water.)

The British were eventually able to make inroads into the fur trading business by undercutting the French by paying higher prices for the furs and providing the Natives with more trade goods, as well as unapologetically providing the Natives with more alcohol.

After a great deal of effort and huge quantities of alcohol, the British were able to gain control of the majority of the Upper Midwest fur trading territory and Mackinaw trading posts. The British used whatever methods they could employ to secure the fur trade, which continued long after the American Revolution.

From the very beginning, when the French traders first showed up in North America, the fur trade life centered on the French Canadian settlements along the St. Lawrence River, with the primary suppliers of fur being the Huron tribes. European markets could not get enough furs. From that hunger, a new breed of French trader emerged referred to as "voyageurs." These rugged men would venture out into the woods looking for beaver pelts and Natives to trade with, becoming hugely successful and, in many cases, very rich. The voyageurs were often gone for two to three years, collecting many bundles of furs. There is one report of a voyageur who returned from a two-year trip with more than one hundred canoes loaded with bundles of precious pelts.

Of all the fur-bearing animals in North American, the beaver was the most prized. The beaver was so highly regarded that its very likeness would eventually show up stamped into the back side of the Canadian nickel.

BEFORE THE EUROPEANS ARRIVED in Canada and the Great Lakes region, it was estimated that more than 10 million beavers lived in the North American wilds. Originally, the Natives hunted them using sharpened sticks, stone hatchets, and spears with fluted arrowheads. As trade with Europeans increased, the Natives became equipped with much better weapons made of steel, as well as, of course, guns. The beaver became an easy target.

Between 1615 and the 1860s, it is estimated that more than 4 million pelts of one kind or another were shipped to the European markets each year. The early 1800s saw the beaver heading for certain extinction. Luckily, European fashion trends changed, with the silk hat becoming more fashionable, causing the demand for beaver pelts to dry up almost entirely.

The beaver had its heyday. When the beaver pelt trade first started, the people in Europe did not think of the beaver as an animal, only as a hat. They even thought the beaver hat had magical powers. They believed that if you rubbed beaver oil into your hair, it would help your memory and improve lost hearing; some believed that the beaver oil would make men more virile. It is well documented by historians that the demand for beaver hats was *the* driving force behind the creation of the colony of New France in Canada.

The beaver fur itself has two different kinds of hair: a short, thick, soft, wooly hair intermixed with a longer, coarse hair. When the pelt is properly pressed, the hairs would interlock, making a solid fabric. This process was called "felting." The most popular furs were from young beavers, which had the softest and thickest fur. Beavers do not hibernate, so their furs get very thick in the winter to keep them warm. Therefore, most beaver trapping was done in the winter.

Another favorite of French traders were the beaver pelts that were worn by the Natives. These furs were worn for the better part of a year or until most of the long hairs on the pelt had been worn off. This pelt was called "coat beaver" and commanded the very highest price on the fur market.

Fur became an item of great economic importance to the development of America, but it was politically important as well. The existence of New France (Canada) depended on the profits of the fur trade. France was not going to spend money on an unproductive outpost, and it was fur that kept New France solvent. The beaver became a factor of empire, and battles were fought and treaties delayed over who was to control access to prime trapping areas. The security and success of the North American fur trade was going to depend on the beaver trap as much as the muskets and bayonets.

BY 1756, THE FUR trade had become so well established that it survived the upheaval of the French and Indian War with very little notice. The routes to the west continued to run from Hudson's Bay, where an English company was dominant; from New York City up to Albany and out past the Great Lakes to the Illinois country; and, the greatest route of all, from Montreal up the Ottawa River, out across Georgian Bay and the Great Lakes, past the settlement of Grand Portage to the river systems in the very heart of the continent.

After their victory in the French and Indian War, the British ran the fur trade largely as their predecessors had done, with only minor adjustments. From the eastern depots came the annual fleet of New York–built canoes, each holding men and more than four tons of goods for use and for trading. At the western end of the Great Lakes, the New York canoes were replaced by northern canoes that were restyled, allowing the traders to penetrate farther into the wilderness, where they wintered and traded with the Natives. As the ice broke up in the spring, the trappers from the west would head for Grand Portage with their furs. There they met their eastern partners with European goods, where they held their annual trapper/trader reunion, during which they would drink, fight, challenge each other to wrestling matches, dance, feast, and settle personal accounts for the year.

In 1674, after the English took complete control of the New Amsterdam area, later to become New York, Dutch and Swedish settlers were taken up and incorporated into the English colonies. The Dutch and Swedes stepped back from the day-to-day trading with Native tribes, leaving the French, English, and Spanish as the three powers to vie for control of North America.

The political and social landscape of North America became more unstable as European wars extended into the New World. In these conflicts, Native Americans were usually allied with either the French or English, depending on who they thought would win or who would benefit them the most. The introduction of European firearms significantly changed the dynamics of the relationship between Europeans and Native Americans.

Three major conflicts shaped New France, the English colonies, and their interactions with Native Americans that took place before 1754:

- King William's War (1688–99)
- Queen Anne's War (1702–13)
- King George's War (1744–48)

Each of these wars was part of a larger war that started in Europe and spread to North America. The final conflict for control of North America started in 1754 and is simply known as the French and Indian War.

For more than a century, Michigan's economic life centered on the fur trade. French visitors, including Antoine de la Mothe Cadillac, marveled at the expanse and potential that the Great Lakes watershed had to offer. Observations of the tribal communities and the environmental suitability for travel led to the expansion of the fur trade, an industry that became vital to both Indigenous peoples and European newcomers.

The basin watershed was interconnected by rivers and portages that connected the St. Lawrence Seaway to the Mississippi River. The main fur trade route ventured west from Montreal, beginning at a portage around the Lachine Rapids of the St. Lawrence River and then up the Ottawa to the Mattawa, across Lake Nipissing, and down the French River to Lake Huron's Georgian Bay and on across to the Mackinac Straits.

From the seventeenth to the nineteenth centuries, Michigan's commerce relied on these maritime routes, which reached their peak with the American Fur Company. Europeans necessarily relied on Indigenous knowledge of the maritime geography to navigate the complicated waterways. Newcomers also adopted Indigenous birch-bark canoes, which were described as "riding on the water with the ease of a sea-bird."

A wide array of explorers, missionaries, fur traders, and imperial officials took careful note of travel in the Great Lakes. Pierre Charlevoix wrote of his trip through the lakes in 1720, "[I]f one always travelled, as I did then, with a clear sky, and a charming climate, on a water as clear as the finest fountain...one would be tempted to travel all one's life."

From 1600 to 1763, traders in the Great Lakes were mostly French, bartering with the Ottawa, Huron, and Algonquian tribes. The trade itself was centered near the French Canadian settlements along the St. Lawrence River. The introduction of the Hudson Bay Company further changed the industry dynamics. Because the rivers were efficient waterways, the English built forts along the coastline, turning the focus away from French Canada. The Great Lakes fur trade dominated the economy in the northwest for more than two centuries.

The American Fur Company held a monopoly on fur trade throughout the Great Lakes, with the company headquarters on Mackinac Island and a branch in Detroit. The Michilimackinac location was very advantageous for trade, positioned between the three Great Lakes of Superior, Michigan, and Huron.

Michilimackinac, Mackinac Island, Detroit, and Sault Ste. Marie were important location points for the fur trade. The Soo acted as a crucial hub for trading posts that extended from the St. Lawrence Seaway throughout the Great Lakes and up into Canada, where the Hudson Bay Company traded. Michilimackinac and Mackinac Island were key stoppage points for exchange, and the port of Detroit controlled access to the Upper Great Lakes from Ontario.

Many different museums in the region have a significant collection of manifests, bills of lading, clearance papers guaranteeing protection for vessels bound to and from Canada, documents certifying duties paid on entering goods, and other papers relating to commodities entering or departing from Michilimackinac. Many of the commodities listed in these documents, prior to 1812, were entered or shipped out on behalf of the American Fur

Company (AFC) through its various agents. Dating from 1838 to 1847, the AFC papers provide detailed information on commerce, domestic and foreign markets, domestic manufacturers, transportation, and the problems encountered by AFC agents in the field.

The fur trade under the AFC was persistent until the 1840s. The AFC Voyageur Contracts Database contains 32,414 contracts signed between the years 1700 and 1822. John Jacob Astor hired hundreds of fur traders from 1817 to the 1830s. Contracts were usually for a three-year period and often meant long journeys from one lake to another. By 1825, the AFC was mostly operating out of Lake Michigan and Lake Superior.

The Michilimackinac area served as a local AFC headquarters, with Fort Detroit as another strategic stopping point. From 1829 to 1831, the AFC harvested approximately 708,000 furs from the far Upper Midwest and Great Lakes region; a decade later, the company harvested 589,000 furs from the Great Lakes region alone. The trade finally started to decline with the introduction of American agriculture, which, unlike Native agriculture, did not work in tandem with the fur trade. As the fur trade gave way to settler colonial expansion in the nineteenth century, changing transportation technologies from water to roads, new national borders, and new visions for the landscape of the Old Northwest and Upper Canada altered the reliance these newcomers had on older modes of movement.

Some historians have tried to focus on the Native American role in the fur trade, especially among Native women. "Furs and Female Kin Networks: The World of Marguerite Magdelaine LaFramboise" illustrates LaFramboise's life as the wife of two fur traders at Fort St. Joseph at Niles, Michigan. Also, the book *Indian Women and French Men: Rethinking Cultural Encounters in the Western Great Lakes* provides a perspective on the fur trade world that places more emphasis on kinship, the primary focus being the role that Native women played in the sociocultural changes within the fur trade, and there were many.

During its heyday, the North American fur trading commerce enjoyed huge successes. The trapping was fantastic for those willing to put in the extraordinarily hard work, and the trading was for many a financial windfall and proved to be a great boon to the European fashion industry.

The trapping and trading industry was made up of hundreds of people, large and small operations, collecting and selling the fine pelts. Their individual stories are amazing and exciting. However, for the purposes of this book, the lives of three prominent trappers/traders will be covered: John Jacob Astor, John Johnston, and Madame Marguerite Magdelaine Marcotte-LaFramboise.

JOHN JACOB ASTOR (1763–1848)

John Jacob Astor was the third son of a German butcher. He was born in Walldorf, Germany. His father was prone to long periods of laziness, while his mother was industrious and frugal. The eldest son, George, moved to England, where he established a musical instrument business. The second son, Henry, moved to New York City, where he became a butcher. John Jacob remained in Germany until 1780. By then, his mother had died, and relations between John and his new stepmother became strained.

Young John Astor worked his way down the Rhine River on a timber barge. By the time he reached salt water, he had saved enough money for the passage to London, where he worked for his brother George making musical instruments. He mastered the English language and listened to all the stories of the rebellious American colonies. By the end of the American Revolution, Astor had saved enough money to buy passage to the new United States of America. He sailed for America with twenty-five dollars, seven of his handmade flutes and a berth on the ship in the crew's quarters.

The ship entered Chesapeake Bay in late January 1784 and became frozen in the ice for two months. Astor used that time to talk with another German emigrant who had been to North America before and had some success in the fur industry. By the time the ice had melted, Astor was sure that the fur trade was what he wanted to do.

John Jacob Astor became hugely wealthy in the fur business without ever setting a single animal trap. He arrived in New York in March 1784, and upon his arrival, he was more determined than ever to make his fortune.

In 1785, he married Sarah Todd. The Todds were one of the original Old Dutch families of New York. She brought with her to the marriage a $300 dowry and a keen sense of business, with an expert eye for furs. With the help of his wife's dowry, Astor opened a musical instrument store in 1786, where he also bought and sold furs with the help of Sarah.

The Astors had eight children. One was stillborn, one died as a young child, and one was never mentally stable. The Astors tended strictly to business, living frugally and devoting themselves entirely to making money.

Astor often left the shop in the hands of his wife while he went off to the frontier looking for furs.

Within a few years Astor knew the fur trade well and had established connections not only throughout the American northwest territories but also in Montreal, which was the heart of the trade. He gained a great advantage over his competitors in 1796 when the Jay Treaty, between the United States and Great Britain, was signed. The British were already beginning their time-honored practice of seeking American friendship at Canada's expense, and the Canadian fur traders had their fur trading legs cut out from under them with the Jay Treaty.

The Canadians' misfortune was Astor's gain. He and the United States would expand together. Astor not only took over territory that had been closed to the Canadians, but he was also clever enough to make a deal with the Northwest Company so that he could import goods through it. Thanks to the writers of the Jay Treaty, he was able to insert himself into the American end of the Canadian trade. By 1800, Astor was recognized as the leading American merchant in the fur trade and was thought to be worth $250,000. He was still only just beginning.

By that time, Astor was starting to act and look like a comfortable capitalist. He moved into a new house in New York City and established worldwide connections, becoming the very picture of early nineteenth-century American merchant. His horizons were always expanding, at least as far as profits were concerned.

Soon after the turn of the century, he became interested in what was then called the Orient. American ships were just starting their China trade, and Astor, during a visit to London, obtained from a friend a license to trade in any East India Company port. Armed with this mandate, Astor persuaded another friend in New York to join in his venture, and together they sent a trade ship to Canton, China. When it returned successfully, Astor's share of the profit was $50,000. New opportunities were opening up before him, although fur was still his primary interest. Part of his profit from the venture into China went into the purchase of real estate in New York City, property that later proved to be the real basis of the Astor fortune.

John Jacob Astor capitalized on the 1803 Louisiana Purchase to expand his fur business from Illinois to the Pacific. His American Fur Company traded furs all the way out to Guangzhou in China. Some thought that the Louisiana Purchase of 1803 was ill-advised for the young republic, but Astor did not share that thinking. With that new immense territory under U.S. control, it became possible to see the fur trade extending all the way to the Pacific coast. The return of the Lewis and Clark Expedition in 1806 added fuel to his ambition, and by the next year, Astor and his agents were fighting to drive the Canadian fur traders out of the upper Mississippi Valley.

Early in his business life, and with the permission of President Thomas Jefferson, Astor established the American Fur Company on April 6, 1808. These were the years of his peak activity with AFC. His Columbia River trading post at Fort Astoria, established in April 1811, was the first U.S. community on the Pacific coast. He financed the overland Astor Expedition in 1810–12 to reach the outpost. Members of the expedition were to discover South Pass, through which hundreds of thousands of settlers on the Oregon, Mormon, and California Trails later used to pass through the Rocky Mountains.

Astor's fur trading ventures were disrupted during the War of 1812, when the British captured his trading posts. In 1816, he joined the opium smuggling trade. His American Fur Company purchased ten tons of European-produced opium and shipped the contraband to Canton, China, onboard the ship *Macedonian*. Astor later left the Chinese opium trade and sold opium solely in Britain.

Astor's fur trading business rebounded in 1817 after the U.S. Congress passed a protectionist law that barred foreign fur traders from U.S. territories. The American Fur Company came to dominate trading in the area around the Great Lakes, absorbing all competitors in a monopoly centered on Mackinac Island.

In 1822, Astor established the Robert Stuart House on Mackinac Island as headquarters for the reorganized American Fur Company, making the island a metropolis of the fur trade. Astor's commercial connections extended over the entire globe, and his ships were found in every sea. Astor's original fur storage sheds are still on the island.

Astor began buying small parcels of land in New York City in 1799 and eventually acquired sizable holdings along the waterfront. After the start of the nineteenth century, flush with profits from the fur trade and his China ventures, he became more systematic, ambitious, and calculating by investing in New York real estate. In 1803, he bought a seventy-acre farm on which he built the Astor Mansion at Hellgate.

In the 1830s, Astor sold his interests in the American Fur Company, as well as all his other China ventures, and used the money to buy and develop large tracts of Manhattan real estate. Astor correctly predicted the city's rapid growth northward on Manhattan Island.

At the time of his death in 1848, Astor was the wealthiest person in the United States, leaving an estate estimated to be worth $20 million, or 0.9 percent of estimated U.S. GDP at the time. (It would be equivalent to $675 million in 2024.) The name John Jacob Astor is well known throughout the world and synonymous with wealth that surpasses the imagination.

Astor is buried at the Trinity Church Cemetery in Manhattan.

John Johnston (1762–1828)

Johnston was born in 1762 in Belfast, Ireland, to an upper-class Scotch-Irish family. His father was a civil engineer who planned and built the Belfast Water Works. During John's youth, his mother's brother was attorney general of Ireland.

Johnston immigrated to Canada in 1792 for what he hoped would be better opportunities. He had letters of introduction to Lord Dorchester, governor of the Canadian colony. Through him, Johnston met leaders in society, including the magnates of the recently formed North West Company in Montreal. The fur trade looked like a good opportunity to make a profit. Johnston planned to be a "wintering partner," one who traded with Native Americans at a frontier post in the interior of the territory. Then with his own capital, he purchased trade goods in Montreal to take with him.

Johnston went to Sault Ste. Marie, a journey that took several weeks, where he settled on the south side of the river, in present-day Michigan. There Johnston met his future wife, Ozhaguscodaywayquay ("Woman of the Green Glade"), daughter of Waubojeeg ("White Fisher"), a prominent Ojibwa chief and leader from what is now northern Wisconsin. Johnston fell in love with Chief Waubojeeg's daughter, but the chief was skeptical of white men. He initially refused when Johnston asked for his daughter's hand in marriage, saying, "White Man, I have noticed your behavior, it has been correct; but, White Man, your color is deceitful. Of you, may I expect better things? You say you are going to Montreal; go, and if you return I shall be satisfied of your sincerity and will give you my daughter." When Johnston returned from Montreal, the couple married, after which his wife took and used the Anglican name of Susan Johnston.

John Johnston and his wife, Susan, became influential leaders in both the Euro-American and Ojibwa communities, although their married life was disrupted by the War of 1812, during which he served on the side of the British. After the war, the U.S. government prohibited fur trading by Canadians in U.S. territory. Johnston was considered Canadian primarily because he had never applied for U.S. citizenship.

Like Johnston, most fur traders were Europeans of social standing, and together with the upper-class Ojibwa women they married, they formed the upper tier of a two-class frontier society. Kinship and ties of affinity proved more than merely useful to the traders. They were both a source of power and a necessity if one was to achieve success in the trade. Johnston was believed to be the first permanent European settler in Sault Ste. Marie.

John Johnston may have been an Irishman by birth, but his lifelong allegiance was to the English territory of Canada. He had been trapping and trading animal furs in Canada and Michigan even before the War of 1812. Due to his prominent role in the fur trade, he would become a leader in the new Michigan Territory, but he would never actually become a U.S. citizen.

The Johnstons' cedar log house on Water Street in Sault Ste. Marie was built in 1796 in the French colonial style. When their eldest daughter, Jane, married Henry Schoolcraft, the U.S. Indian agent, the Johnstons built extra room onto their home for the Schoolcrafts to live in. Some years later, the Schoolcrafts built their own house in the village. The addition the Johnstons had built is now the only remaining part of the Johnston house, and it is one of the most historic houses in the city.

Although the south side of the St. Mary's River became U.S. territory in 1797 after treaty settlements following the end of the American Revolutionary War, Johnston still refused to become a U.S. citizen. At the time, the border was very much a fluid area. In those years, North American Natives had a separate status and were generally not considered U.S. citizens.

As a young man, Johnston was thrilled at the opportunity he saw with the North West Company. He was impressed by the partners he met and their refined lives. When it was formed in 1787, the company had twenty-three partners and nearly two thousand employees, made up of agents, factors, clerks, guides, interpreters, and voyageurs.

As part of their lifestyle of building relationships, the Johnstons welcomed to their home an array of significant players in the region, including surveyors, explorers, traders, governmental officials, trappers, and political leaders. With his wife, Johnston developed a broad knowledge of both the Ojibwa ways and the geography of the Great Lakes region. He played an integral role in developing the Michigan frontier after being appointed to the post of justice of the peace, even though he never became a U.S. citizen.

Sault Ste. Marie, on the south side of the river, was a community with a mix of fur traders, most of whom had Native American wives; Ojibwas, some of high status; and workers who were European, Native American, and Métis.

The community also included permanent and temporary structures, like warehouses for furs, scattered housing, Native wigwams, and sheds for boats. Many of the Ojibwas stayed in the area for the fishing more than for the settlement or the desire to be around white people.

The increasing economic tensions between Great Britain and the United States affected the fur trade. In 1806, the U.S. government requested changes to the Jay Treaty of 1794 that restricted British fur traders to operating only in Canada.

During the War of 1812, Johnston assisted the British due to his long-standing affiliations with them. After a direct appeal from the British garrison at Fort Mackinac, Johnston supplied about one hundred of his men and took two bateaux of supplies for their relief in 1814. An American force failed to intercept him, and it continued on to Sault Ste. Marie. There the U.S. raiders burned the North West Company warehouses on both sides of the St. Mary's River, causing substantial fur losses to Johnston and his company. The troops also raided his house, Johnston Hall. They looted the library and furnishings and set fire to the house. Johnston's wife and children fled into the woods when the soldiers arrived.

After the war, John Johnston made a direct appeal to the governor of Michigan, Lewis Cass, to lift the restriction against his trading in U.S. territory because of his other services to the region. Governor Cass refused. Johnston claimed that he suffered financially from the losses due to reduced trading and was never able to rebuild his former wealth. Although he applied to the British government for compensation for his losses, no payment was made. Believing that he was too old to move to Canada, he stayed in his home in Sault Ste. Marie, Michigan. In 1821, Johnston served as a commissioner during negotiations to end the rivalry between the North West and Hudson Bay Companies and helped achieve their merger.

Still worried about potential British agitation of Native Americans along the border, in 1822 the U.S. government built and staffed Fort Brady at Sault Ste. Marie. With the fort and troops, other American settlers started to come into the area in greater number. With that, the culture of Sault Ste. Marie changed quickly. Johnston and others who had earlier formed and dominated the community were totally ignored by the newcomers as they banded together. The presence of military troops formalized the role of government. The new American residents were reluctant to become involved with the French, Ojibwas, or Métis and disdained most of that existing society.

The Johnstons had eight children, most of whom were American by the time of their births in that city. They were educated in English, Ojibwa, and French. Johnston had a large library filled with English classical authors, including poets, which his children used for their literary education. The Johnstons took care to educate their children in both European and Native American cultures and expected them to have opportunities in society equivalent to their standing. Many other fur traders instead sent their children to Montreal for formal education.

The Johnstons' eldest daughter, Jane, married Henry Rowe Schoolcraft, who arrived in Sault Ste. Marie in 1822 as Indian agent for the U.S. government. He would go on to establish formal relationships with the Native Americans in the region. He became noted as an ethnographer and writer about Native American life.

In 2008, Jane Johnston Schoolcraft was posthumously inducted into the Michigan Women's Hall of Fame for her own contributions to literature and history. She is recognized as the first Native American literary writer and poet. A major collection of her work was published in 2007.

After John Johnston's death in 1828, Susan Johnston and their son William managed the maple sugaring and fishing business on Sugar Island, a Michigan island in the St. Mary's River. Their youngest son, John McDougall Johnston, settled permanently on Sugar Island. He was later appointed as the last official Indian agent in the area.

MARGUERITE MAGDELAINE MARCOT-LAFRAMBOISE (1780–1846)

Marguerite Magdelaine Marcot was born in February 1780 at Fort St. Joseph, near the present-day city of Niles, Michigan. She was the youngest daughter of the seven Métis children of Jean Baptiste Marcot and his Ottawa wife, Marie Nekesh Amighissen. Marie's maternal grandfather was Chief Kewinoquot of the Ottawa tribe.

Jean Baptiste Marcot was a French fur trader and chief agent for the Northwest Fur Company. He was murdered in 1783 by Native Americans at the portage between the Fox and Washington Rivers.

The two youngest of the seven children, Marguerite and Therese, were baptized as Roman Catholic on Mackinac Island on August 1, 1786. The children were raised in their mother's culture and learned several languages. Their father, prior to his death, made arrangements for his children to go to Montreal to be educated. After his death, their widowed mother did not have the resources to do that.

Marguerite Magdelaine Marcot married Joseph LaFramboise in 1794. On September 24, 1795, she gave birth to their first child, a girl they named Josette LaFramboise. Their son Joseph LaFramboise was born in March 1805. Although Magdelaine and Joseph had been married by Ottawa custom, they had their married solemnized by a Catholic missionary on Mackinac Island on July 11, 1804, at which time she became known as Madame LaFramboise.

Joseph LaFramboise developed his fur-trading business in what today is known as the Grand River Valley of western Michigan. Joseph, along with his wife, Marguerite, would transport their trade goods from Mackinac Island to the Grand River area every fall, in order to trade and secure most furs from the local tribes. As a partnership, they were very successful in building their reputations as dependable, honest traders. They soon became successful enough to build another trading post in the area of today's Fallsburg, Michigan. Every spring, they returned to Mackinac Island with the furs they had acquired through the season's trading.

Joseph LaFramboise was murdered in 1806 by a Native American unhappy with a trade the two made. Madame LaFramboise took over their fur trade. She continued to manage several trading posts and expanded her business throughout the western and northern portions of Michigan's Lower Peninsula. She also raised their two children, sending both Josette and Joseph to Montreal for education in French schools.

Madame Marguerite Magdelaine Marcot-LaFramboise became one of the most successful fur traders in the Northwest Territory of the United States, in the area of present-day western Michigan, even against the competition of John Jacob Astor.

Madame LaFramboise soon owned a string of trading posts in Michigan's Grand River Valley. Although she was reputed to be no ordinary woman, Madame LaFramboise has been historically mistreated. She had been very successful in an exclusively male trade. During this period, an experienced fur trader earned about $1,000 per year (a very large sum at the time). LaFramboise was highly successful, sometimes earning between $5,000 and $10,000 per year.

Madame LaFramboise founded a school on Mackinac Island for Native American children. She also supported a Sunday school and other activities at the Catholic Sainte Anne Church. Honored as one of the most prominent early businesswomen of the new state, she was elected posthumously to the recently established Michigan Women's Hall of Fame in 1984.

In later years, Magdelaine's older sisters, Therese and Catherine, married and also became active in the fur trade; they took over from their husbands, George Schindler and Jean Baptiste Cadotte, respectively. Although neither became as well known as Magdelaine, they were upwardly mobile, making good lives for themselves and their descendants. The descendants of Therese Schindler became prominent in Wisconsin medical and social circles. The women used their family ties among the Ottawa and knowledge about the varieties of regional Native American tribes and culture to build and maintain their businesses. Like Magdelaine in later years, Therese Schindler was based mostly on Mackinac Island.

In the early 1800s, Mackinac Island had a permanent population of about 250. Although it was part of the United States and a territory, most of the residents were still of French and Métis ancestry, and French was the predominant language. In the summer trading season, the population could reach 4,000.

Magdelaine and her sisters became friendly with Elizabeth (Bertrand) Mitchell and her husband. She was the mixed-race wife of the Scottish physician David Mitchell. He had served since 1774 as an officer with the British at Michilimackinac, where they had married. He was part of the Eighth Footman Regiment, which departed Mackinac Island after the American Revolutionary War. Mitchell chose to resign his commission and stay on Mackinac Island with his wife and children.

Because Madame LaFramboise spoke several regional Native American languages, in addition to French and English, and had a strong network among the Native Americans, she continued to be successful. In about 1818, she became an affiliate of Astor's and finally sold her fur business to his American Fur Company in 1822. Rix Robinson, a Michigan pioneer, purchased her other business operations. LaFramboise, then forty-one years old and a very wealthy woman, retired to a stately home on Mackinac Island. Her son-in-law Captain Benjamin Pierce, commandant of Fort Mackinac, personally oversaw the construction of her new home.

After her retirement from fur trading, LaFramboise taught herself to read and write in both French and English. She supported the first Catholic school for Native American children on Mackinac Island, starting it in her home.

Continuing her devotion to Ste. Anne's Church there, she taught catechism to the parish's children. She was influential in keeping the congregation together in the several years when it did not have a regular priest. Both her activism with the church and work for the education of children secured her a respected place in Mackinac society.

After retiring from the fur trade, Madame LaFramboise had a fine home built (some may call it a mansion) on Mackinac Island. The home still stands next door to Ste. Anne's Church today. The mansion has been acquired, renovated, and adapted for use as the modern-day Harbour View Inn.

Madame Marguerite Magdalene Marcot-LaFramboise died on April 4, 1846. Father Henri Van Renterghen of Ste. Anne's honored the request of Madame LaFramboise and had her interred beneath the altar of the church. In the 1960s, Ste. Anne's was renovated and a basement activity center was added. The remains of LaFramboise, as well as those of her daughter Josephine Pierce and her infant daughter Josette, who had been buried with her, were relocated and interred in Ste. Anne's churchyard. A historic marker there also recognizes LaFramboise and her contributions.

In the early twenty-first century, Ste. Anne's Church constructed a crypt in the church for interment and prayer. It honored LaFramboise by reinterring her and her family's remains in the crypt on July 26, 2013. Some of her descendants attended the ceremony.

BIBLIOGRAPHY

Adamich, Tom, Archivist, Greening Nursery. "The Wayne Stockade." 1993.

Armour, David A. "David and Elizabeth: The Mitchell Family of the Straits of Mackinac." *Mackinac History* 2, leaflet 6 (1982).

———. "Made in Mackinac: Crafts at Fort Michilimackinac." *Mackinac History*, leaflet 8 (1966).

Baird, Willard. *This Is Our Michigan*. Federated Publications, 1954.

Bald, F. Clever. *Michigan in Four Centuries*. Harper Publishing, 1954.

Caruso, John Anthony. *The Great Lakes Frontier: A Epic of the Old Northwest*. Bobbs-Merrill & Company, 1961.

Catton, Bruce. *Michigan: A Bicentennial History*. W.W. Norton & Company, 1984.

Chase, Lew Allen. "Fort Wilkins, Copper Harbor, Michigan." *Michigan History Magazine* 4 (1920): 608. Michigan Historical Commission.

Cunningham, Wilbur M. *Land of Four Flags*. Gilliam Eerdmans Publishing, 1961.

Detroit Historical Society. "Timeline of Detroit: Founding of Detroit." May 11, 2024.

De Vauban, Sébastien Le Prestre. *The New Method of Fortification as Practiced by M. de Vauban, Engineer-General of France. Together with a New Treatise of Geometry*. 5th ed. London: Book Division, 1748.

Dunnigan, Brian Leigh. "Fort Holmes." *Reports on Mackinac and Archeology*, no. 10 (1984). Mackinac Island State Park Commission.

Eccles, W.J. "The Fur Trade and Eighteenth-Century Imperialism." *William and Mary Quarterly* 40, no. 3 (1983): 342–62.

Eccles, William J. *Frontenac: The Courtier Governor*. Mclelland & Stewart, 1957.

Encyclopedia of Detroit. "French Detroit (1700–1760)." Detroit Historical Society, May 11, 2024.

Endlich, Helen. *History of Port Huron*. Published by author, 1981.

Farmer, Silas. *History of Detroit & Wayne County and Early Michigan*. Detroit Publishing for Munsell & Company, 1890.

"Fort Gratiot." *Michigan History Magazine* 4, no. 1 (January 1920): 141–55.

"Fort Michilimackinac." *American Heritage Magazine* (August–September 1978).

Fowle, Otto. *Sault Ste. Marie*. G.P. Putnam & Sons, 1925.

Gerin-Lajoie, Marie, trans. "Fort Michilimackinac in 1749, Lotbiniere's Plan and Description." *Mackinac History* 2, leaflet 5 (1976).

Haight, Floyd L. *History of the Dearborn Historical Museum*. Vol. 1. January 1961.

Hamil, Fred C. *Michigan in the War of 1812*. Michigan Historical Commission-Lansing, 1960.

Havard, Giles. *The Great Peace of 1701*. MacGill-Queen's University Press, 2001.

Havighurst, Walter. *Three Flags at the Straits: The Forts of Mackinac*. Prentice Hall Publishing, 1966.

Hull, William, and James Grant Forbes. *Report of the Trial of Brigadier General William Hull, Commanding the Northwestern Army of the United States; by Court-Martial Held at Albany on Monday, 3d, January, 1814*. Eastburn, Kirk and Company, 1814.

Hutchison, Craig, Kimberly Rising, and the Dearborn Historical Museum. *Dearborn, Michigan*. Arcadia Publishing, 2002.

Internet Archive. "Commandant's Quarters, Dearborn Arsenal." Archived April 21, 2009.

Kent, Timothy J. *Rendezvous at the Straits: Fur Trade and Military Activities at Fort de Buade and Fort Michilimackinac, 1669–1781*. Silver Fox Enterprises; 2004.

Lewis, Ferris E. *Detroit: A Wilderness Outpost of Old France*. Wayne University Press, 1951.

———. *My State and Its History*. Hillsdale School Supply Company, 1955.

May, George, and Herbert Brinks. *A Michigan Reader: 11,000 B.C. to A.D. 1865*. Eerdmans Publishing, 1974.

May, George S. "The Askin Inventory: A Mackinac Businessman's Property in 1778." *Mackinac History*, leaflet 2 (1963). Mackinac Island State Park Commission.

Miles, Richard D. *The Stars and Stripes Come to Detroit*. Wayne University Press, 1951.

National Park Service. National Register Information System. March 13, 2009.

———. National Register of Historic Places—Fort Wayne. March 13, 2009.

Pasquelle, Ethel Rowan. *When Michigan Was Young*. Eerdmans Publishing, 1950.

Radike, Floyd. *Detroit: A French Village on the Frontier*. Wayne University Press, 1951.

Simmons, David A. "Military Architecture on the American Frontier." Inventory and Registration Historic Preservation Division, Ohio Historical Society.

Skinner, Claiborne A. *The Upper Country: French Enterprise in the Colonial Great Lakes.* Johns Hopkins University Press, 2008.

Stevens, Wayne E. "The Organization of the British Fur Trade, 1760–1800." *Mississippi Valley Historical Review* 3, no. 2 (1916): 172–202.

Stone, Lyle M. "Archaeology at Fort Michilimackinac." Mackinac Island State Park Commission, leaflet no. 9 (1967).

Turgeon, Laurier. "French Fishers, Fur Traders, and Amerindians during the Sixteenth Century: History and Archaeology." *William and Mary Quarterly* 55, no. 4 (1998): 585–610.

Wikipedia. "American Revolutionary War Forts." Updated July 9, 2024. https://en.wikipedia.org/wiki/Category:American_Revolutionary_War_forts.

———. "Fort Wayne (Indiana fort)." https://en.wikipedia.org/wiki/Fort_Wayne_(Indiana_fort).

———. "Fort Wilkins Historic State Park." https://en.wikipedia.org/wiki/Fort_Wilkins_Historic_State_Park#Fort_Wilkins.

ABOUT THE AUTHOR

David Wedge is a graduate of Lake Superior State University and is a retired engineer with a lifelong passion for Michigan history. He is a native Michigander who, along with his wife, splits time between Michigan and Florida.